Faust
theater of the world

❡

Twayne's Masterwork Studies
Robert Lecker, General Editor

Faust
theater of the world

¶

Jane K. Brown

Twayne Publishers • New York
Maxwell Macmillan Canada • Toronto
Maxwell Macmillan International • New York Oxford Singapore Sydney

Twayne's Masterwork Studies No. 96

Copyright 1992 by Twayne Publishers

Twayne Publishers
Macmillan Publishing Company
866 Third Avenue
New York, New York 10022

Maxwell Macmillan Canada, Inc.
1200 Eglinton Avenue East
Suite 200
Don Mills, Ontario M3C 3N1

Macmillan Publishing Company is a part of the Maxwell Communication Group of Companies.

Library of Congress Cataloging-in-Publication Data

Brown, Jane K., 1943–
Faust : theater of the world / by Jane K. Brown.
p.   cm. — (Twayne's masterwork studies ; no. 96)
Includes bibliographical references and index.
ISBN 0-8057-9407-7 (cloth). — ISBN 0-8057-8557-4 (pbk.)
1. Goethe, Johann Wolfgang von, 1749–1832. Faust. I. Title. II. Series.
PT1925.B75   1992
832'.6—dc20
92-6896
CIP

The paper used in this publication meets the minimum requirements of American National Standard for Information Sciences Permanence of Paper for Printed Library Materials, ANSI Z39.48-1984.

10 9 8 7 6 5 4 3 2 1 (alk. paper)

10 9 8 7 6 5 4 3 2 1 (pbk.: alk. paper)

Printed in the United States of America.

contents

note on the references and acknowledgments

Faust was originally published in two parts that are still often read separately. The second part is a masterpiece of equal stature to the first. It elaborates and unfolds the issues developed in Part I, revealing not only what was already implicit but also the further development of Goethe's thinking and his reactions to the changes in European society between 1800 and 1830. There is no question that Part I can be read on its own with great profit, as probably can Part II. Nevertheless, I encourage any reader who finds Part I interesting to take on Part II; it operates in a stylistic mode that may seem uncomfortable at first but is exhilarating for those who meet its challenge. It contains some of the most beautiful poetry ever written in German.

In an introductory study of this sort, there is not space to reconstruct the process of interpretation by examining each segment, or even selected passages, in detail. The extended analysis on which the arguments in this book rest may be found in my *Goethe's Faust: The German Tragedy* (Ithaca, N.Y.: Cornell University Press, 1986).

Most readers of this book will be studying *Faust* in translation. The many translations available have different strengths and limitations, and none can be considered definitive. Several are listed in the bibliography. To avoid confusion, I provide in this book my own literal translations of quotations from one of the most widely used editions of *Faust*, that prepared by Erich Trunz (Hamburg, Germany: Wegner, 1963). These citations are followed by the line numbers of that edition in parentheses. All other translations in the text are also mine.

Note on the References and Acknowledgments

I have had generous assistance from friends and colleagues in preparing this manuscript. I would like to thank Clark Muenzer and D. L. Ashliman for their help with the frontispiece, and Hellmut Ammerlahn, Cyrus Hamlin, Paul Hernadi, Gunter Hertling, Kim Johnson-Bogart, and Sabine Wilke for their careful and helpful readings of the first version of the text. Many of the arguments were sharpened in response to general discussions at a National Endowment for the Humanities Institute on *Faust* at the University of California in the summer of 1990, and in particular in extended discussion with Paul Hernadi and Cyrus Hamlin, who were very generous with their time. My husband, Marshall, has been my severest and most persistent, but also my most patient and supportive, critic; the debt is beyond acknowledgment. The basic line of discussion was shaped by an especially lively and wonderful group of students in a *Faust* class at the University of Washington in the spring of 1989; to them this book is affectionately dedicated.

Johann Wolfgang Goethe. Painting by Angelika Kauffmann, 1787–88. Taken from *Die Bildnisse Goethes,* ed. Ernst Schulte-Strathaus. Propyläen-Ausgabe von Goethes Sämtlichen Werken: Erstes Supplement. Munich: Georg Muller, 1910. Plate 68.

chronology:
Johann Wolfgang Goethe's
life and works

1749   Johann Wolfgang Goethe born 28 August in Frankfurt am Main, free city of the Holy Roman Empire, to Johann Kaspar Goethe, a wealthy patrician, and Katharina Elisabeth Textor Goethe, daughter of the mayor. Only sibling to survive is Cornelia Goethe Schlosser (1750–77).

1755   Education begins under father's direction; eventually includes instruction in Latin, Greek, French, Italian, English, Hebrew, drawing, and history.

1756–1763   Seven Years' War establishes Prussia as a major European power, further undermining the already tottering Holy Roman Empire. During the French occupation of Frankfurt, Goethe enjoys extensive opportunities to see French plays. His family houses Count Thoranc, commandant of the city, who fills the house with local painters. Goethe's father supports Prussia in this war, his grandfather Austria and France.

1757   Writes his first extant poem, a New Year's greeting for his grandparents.

1765–1768   At father's insistence attends university in Leipzig to study law. Spends more time in literature and drawing classes and in informal literary activity. Serious illness forces his return home. Writes his first extant play, pastoral comedy *The Wayward Lover*.

1769–1770   Studies alchemy and mysticism with Susanne von Klettenberg, friend of his mother.

1770–1771   Completes legal studies in Strasbourg. Spends more time attending lectures on medicine and pursuing literary activity with Johann Gottfried Herder, who stimulates Goethe's lifelong enthusiasm for Homer, Shakespeare, Sterne, Goldsmith, and folk song.

1771   Enters legal practice in Frankfurt and becomes important figure in Sturm und Drang (storm and stress) movement, a loose group of rebellious young writers trying to free German literature from the hegemony of French neoclassicism. Begins historical drama in prose, *Götz von Berlichingen with the Iron Hand*.

1773   Publishes *Götz*. Begins *Faust* (continues to work sporadically on it until 1832).

1774   First novel, *The Sorrows of Young Werther*, appears and is banned in Leipzig for immorality. It is an immediate success all over Europe and establishes Goethe's reputation for life. Publishes numerous short satires.

1775   Begins work on historical drama in prose, *Egmont*. In October departs to visit eighteen-year-old Duke Carl August in Weimar, where he will spend the rest of his life—first as the duke's personal friend and hunting companion, then in various ministerial posts (chiefly 1776–88), and later as resident artist, intellectual, and celebrity.

1776   Begins intense platonic relationship with Charlotte von Stein, who is generally credited with taming Goethe's Sturm und Drang energy into his mature classicism.

1777   Begins first version of novel *Wilhelm Meister*, which will occupy him on and off for eighteen years.

1779   Writes first version of *Iphigenia in Tauris* (drama loosely modeled on Euripides), performed at court with Goethe in role of Orestes. Later rewritten in blank verse.

1780	Begins another verse drama, *Torquato Tasso*, about author of Renaissance epic *Jerusalem Redeemed*.
1782	Receives patent of nobility through influence of Duke Carl August; henceforth Johann Wolfgang von Goethe. Father dies.
1784	Discovers intermaxillary bone in man, an important finding in linking human evolution with the great apes. Interest in biology had grown out of work in phrenology with Protestant mystic J. C. Lavater in previous decade.
1785	Diamond Necklace Affair involves French queen Marie Antoinette in scandal and intensifies European concern for stability of French political system. Goethe becomes increasingly interested in both geology and botany.
1786	Departs in secret to visit Italy. Travels incognito and reveals whereabouts only after settling in Rome, where he pursues developing interests in geology and biology, studies drawing, and completes major classical plays *Egmont*, *Iphigenia in Tauris*, and *Torquato Tasso*.
1788	Returns to Weimar a changed man who views himself above all as an artist. Installs his mistress, Christiane Vulpius (1765–1816), a worker in local artificial flower factory, in his house (decisive rupture with Charlotte von Stein in following year).
1789	French Revolution opens 25 years of war, social disruption, and frequent political reorganization across Europe. Dramatist and poet Friedrich Schiller (1759–1805) comes to University of Jena in Duchy of Weimar as professor of history. Christiane bears Goethe's first and only surviving child, Julius August Walther Goethe (1789–1830), on 25 December.
1790	First publication of scenes from *Faust* as *Faust: A Fragment*. Begins serious study of optics.

1792   Unwillingly accompanies Duke Carl August on Allied campaign against France and continues his optical studies during campaign. Allies are stopped at Valmy on 20 September and retreat in disarray.

1793   Accompanies Duke Carl August on successful Allied siege of Mainz. Expresses disgust with contemporary politics in hexameter epic *Reinhard the Fox*. Beginning of Terror in France.

1794   Johann Gottlieb Fichte (1762–1814), leading exponent of Kant's new critical philosophy and developer of German idealism, joins faculty at University of Jena partly as result of Goethe's efforts. For next 10 years Weimar and Jena are the intellectual center of Germany; virtually every significant German philosopher and poet (Hegel, Herder, Hölderlin, Wilhelm and Alexander von Humboldt, Kleist, Novalis, Schelling, A. W. Schlegel, F. Schlegel, Tieck, Wieland) lives there or pays lengthy visits, drawn by the presence of Goethe, Schiller, and Fichte. Goethe and Schiller become close friends and begin collaborating on series of journals and essays. Until Schiller's death in 1805 they support and spur one another to produce their greatest masterpieces.

1795   Scandalizes many readers with *Roman Elegies*, cycle of erotic poems, in Schiller's journal *Die Horen*. Also publishes there *Conversations of German Refugees* (first cycle of novellas in German), and, independently, *Wilhelm Meister's Apprenticeship*, first great European bildungsroman (novel of education).

1796   Writes series of elegies and epigrams in ancient Greek meters.

1797   Resumes work on *Faust* at Schiller's urging, and works sporadically on it until Part I and some passages for Part II are completed by 1806.

1798	Publishes *Hermann and Dorothea*, idyllic epic in Homeric meter on impact of French Revolution and its refugees in Germany. Goethe's most important reaction to the Revolution, it remains his best-loved work into twentieth century. Begins translating Cellini and Diderot, writing extensively on aesthetics, publishing journal on art, and sponsoring annual competitions among German artists. Studies geology and magnetism and begins work on major optical treatise, *Theory of Color* (published 1810), which he will call his greatest achievement.
1799	Napoleon comes to power in France in coup of 18 Brumaire (second month of French Revolutionary calendar).
1799–1805	Intensive involvement with all aspects of court theater in staging his own and Schiller's current work, as well as translations and adaptations by himself, Schiller, and others.
1802	Through translation by August Wilhelm Schlegel, inspired to lifelong enthusiasm for Spanish dramatist Pedro Calderón de la Barca (1600–81), whom he regards as second only to Shakespeare.
1804	Madame de Staël visits Weimar; her book *On Germany* (1810), will popularize the new German literature in France and England.
1805	Schiller dies, leaving Goethe increasingly isolated. End of Goethe's classical period.
1806	French defeat Prussians at battles of Jena and Auerstedt, bringing Holy Roman Empire to an end. In wake of this catastrophe Goethe marries Christiane and legitimizes his son.
1807	Begins work on *Wilhelm Meister's Journeyman Years*, sequel to both *Apprenticeship* and to *Conversations of German Refugees*. Begins cycle of sonnets (completed 1808).

1808	Publishes *Faust: Part I*. Napoleon summons Goethe to discuss *Werther* with him on occasion of Congress of Erfurt and names him to Legion of Honor.
1809	Scandalizes public again with frank treatment of divorce in novel *Elective Affinities*, originally to have been a novella in *Journeyman Years*. Begins work on series of autobiographical works that will continue through 1820s and establish autobiography as a form of historiography.
1811–1814	Publishes first three parts of *Poetry and Truth*, autobiography to 1775 (Part IV published 1833).
1814	Begins writing poems in style of Persian poet Hafis (ca. 1320–ca. 1389), whose work had been recently translated into German.
1815	Napoleon defeated at Waterloo and Europe restored to prerevolutionary boundaries and stability by Congress of Vienna.
1816	Christiane dies.
1817	Publishes *Italian Journey* as continuation of autobiography. Demonstration by liberal students at Wartburg and subsequent condemnation isolate Goethe further from German liberals. Socializes with Prince Metternich, Austrian foreign minister and architect of the Restoration, the following summer.
1819	Publishes *West-Eastern Divan*, collection of poems in Persian style, with extensive annotations on Oriental history and culture.
1821	Publishes first version of *Wilhelm Meister's Journeyman Years*.
1822	Publishes *Campaign in France* and *Siege of Mainz*, memoirs of military experiences in 1792–93.
1823	Writes "Trilogy on Passion," greatest of his many love poems.
1825	Resumes work on *Faust: Part II*.

1827	Writes "Sino-German Hours and Seasons," cycle of poems in Chinese style.
1828	Duke Carl August dies. Publication of "Novella," greatest of Goethe's short prose narratives.
1829	*Faust: Part I* performed for first time—first in Braunschweig and then elsewhere in Germany, including Weimar, in honor of poet's eightieth birthday. Publishes expanded second version of *Wilhelm Meister's Journeyman Years*, dealing with changed social conditions in postrevolutionary Europe.
1830	Son August dies in Rome; leaves three children.
1831	Completes *Faust: Part II* and seals manuscript for publication after his death.
1832	Unseals manuscript to make final revisions. Dies March 22.

Literary and
Historical Context

¶

1

An Age of Revolution

Goethe's work on *Faust* spans the romantic period. When it was begun in 1773 Rousseau, Diderot, and Voltaire were at their height; its completion in 1831 roughly coincided with the deaths of Scott and Byron, and with the first realist masterpieces of Stendhal and Balzac. This was the age when European culture first explicitly confronted the consequences of secularization. In the early eighteenth century there was still a widespread belief that all life is governed by a supernatural order in which everything has its ordained place. By 1830 the material world was increasingly seen as its own justification and principle of being. This shift of value from supernatural to natural, God to man, system to individual, religious to secular institutions was marked by the French and American revolutions, the industrial revolution, and the Kantian revolution in philosophy. A new consciousness of the importance and shape of history appeared in the turn against classical order and in the passion and iconoclasm of romantic literature. These developments are reflected not only in the themes of Goethe's *Faust* but even in the structure and style of the play.

"Here and today begins a new epoch in the history of the world, and you can say you were there,"[1] Goethe told his discouraged fellows on 19 September 1792, after they and the united forces of Central Europe had failed to rout the revolutionary French army. For the first time in Europe a people loyal to an abstract idea of nationhood rather than to a particular ruling family had defeated the traditional order. During the first half of Goethe's life Germany was still officially part of the Holy Roman Empire, which had originated with Charlemagne in 800 A.D. What is now Germany consisted of 300 separate principalities of various sizes, including some 50 independent free cities. The Grand Duchy of Weimar, at 700 square miles, was by no means the smallest, but it was governed as four independent units. Its political unity depended only on its parts happening to have been inherited by the same person, not on any national coherence. The largest states—Bavaria, Saxony, Austria, and Prussia—competed in various combinations for political ascendancy, with Prussia and Austria emerging as the two major German powers by the end of the Seven Years' War (1756–63). All this changed dramatically after 1792. Napoleon made an end to the Holy Roman Empire in 1806, and the succeeding Wars of Liberation left the German states with a powerful desire for national unity, which was finally fulfilled under Prussian leadership in 1870.

In referring to a new epoch, Goethe was probably thinking even more about changes in forms of government than about changes in national boundaries. By midcentury political philosophers of the Enlightenment such as Voltaire, Montesquieu, and Rousseau had generated compelling rationales for more democratic forms of government. At the same time France, which had provided a model to all Europe of a splendid absolute monarchy, deteriorated rapidly in the changing political and economic climate. Goethe and his contemporaries watched scandals involving even the Royal Family, the Revolution of 1789, the succeeding Terror, and finally the rise of Napoleon with consternation and horror, but also with profound ambivalence. After Napoleon's defeat in 1815, the Congress of Vienna attempted to stabilize a simplified version of the prerevolutionary political order, but it left simmering demands for greater democracy all over Europe—demands that exploded into revolution in France in 1830 and everywhere in 1848.

This period also saw the beginnings of the industrial revolution, earlier in England than on the continent. Technological and economic advances fostered both the general sense of human individuality championed by the Enlightenment and the particular desire of the middle class to share political power more explicitly than before. But by 1820 more prescient spirits, Goethe among them, began to see how the industrial revolution undermined the ideology of individual dignity and self-development from which it had grown. Technology speeded up the pace of life and alienated laborers from their work and from their traditional contexts. While Part I of *Faust* portrays the tragic narrowness of the traditional social order, Part II explores the sinister effects of large-scale manipulation of economic forces (i.e., the printing of money and inflation) and of political forces for economic development. Materialism had become both the order and the central problem of the day.

In the later eighteenth century philosophers too began to confront the implications of secularization. Since the mid-seventeenth century thinkers had focused on the individual self, the subject, rather than on God or some transcendent order as the grounding for truth. By Goethe's time philosophers like Hume, Rousseau, and Kant had revealed the inherent difficulty with the new subjectivity. In simplest terms, the more knowledge was grounded in the self, the more uncertain any kind of objective or divine truth outside of the perceiving mind became. The German idealists—Fichte, Schelling, Schleiermacher, and Hegel are the best known—invented different systems to rescue the independent validity of the object in face of the insight that all human knowledge depends on the observer. Fichte was unable to ward off charges of atheism and had to resign his professorship in Jena in 1799, despite Goethe's efforts to mediate. In the late 1780s German philosophers had already engaged in substantial public controversy about whether the seventeenth-century Dutch philosopher Spinoza was a pantheist who considered nature to be divine, and therefore an atheist. The controversy reveals the emotion still attached to the question of whether truth was located in the world or in a transcendent order.

The Spinoza controversy was part of a revival of neoplatonism. The neoplatonism of the romantic period opposed mind or spirit to physical being or world. Spirit is the pole of divinity and order; world is chaotic unless somehow informed by spirit. In the later idealist discussion this neoplatonist opposition merges with the Kantian opposition of subject and object, so that nature, the world, subjectivity, and what Goethe often called the real became aligned against spirit, transcendence, objectivity, and the Goethean ideal. Goethe and his contemporaries were not willing simply to accept materialism, so they tended to relate these oppositions dialectically and to seek some resolution or mediation, often in art. To a large extent *Faust* documents Goethe's participation in this intellectual ferment and represents his own attempt to come to terms with the romantic dialectic of subject and object.

A last important aspect of this philosophical revolution is historicism, which emerged in the later eighteenth century. It is the theory that sociocultural phenomena are historically determined, so that there are no absolute values in human culture. Each period has its own goals and can be understood and evaluated only in its own terms. Since the Renaissance, and to some extent even in the Middle Ages, the classical world (especially Rome) had been the normative ideal for European culture; historicism, however, implied that imitation of antiquity was not a reasonable goal for modern culture, which instead had to be its unique self. It also implied that other nonclassical cultures were just as valid and important as Roman antiquity. While Europeans readily espoused other cultural models—the romantic period saw all kinds of cultural revivals and awakening interest in the Orient, primitive cultures, and the Middle Ages—they found it difficult to relinquish the classical ideal, and more difficult still to identify and practice the unique style of modern culture. *Faust* is at the center of this cultural ferment; it is a work characterized not only by its preoccupation with the themes of time and history but also by the stylistic self-consciousness evident in both its endless parodies of earlier styles and Goethe's attempts to create a unique new form.

Since the idea of a German nation-state was just emerging in Goethe's time, the historicist demand for a specifically modern form combined with the local need for a specifically German form. But romanticism embraced so many other cultures that a conflict developed between its stylistic tolerance and nationalist political goals. The problem is especially acute in *Faust* because it was recognized as the great masterpiece of the new German literature from its earliest drafts, but is simultaneously the single romantic work most open to all of European culture. In all respects, then, from style to its significance for its culture, *Faust* embodies the conflicts of its period.

2

The Importance of the Work

Why should American students read *Faust* today? Goethe was perceived as overwhelmingly important by his contemporaries and by European intellectuals for more than a century after his death. But we are neither Goethe's contemporaries nor European intellectuals of the last century. Given the rapidity with which our world is changing and the diversity of the society in which we must function, why should we read yet another book—a long and difficult one at that—by a dead white European male, to put the question as bluntly as possible? Beyond *Faust*'s impact and representativeness for its time, three other factors come to mind: first, students who read *Faust* today still find it compelling; second, Germany has defined itself as a nation in terms of Goethe's text in many different—and always disturbing—ways over the last century; and, finally, *Faust* raises problems of knowing, identity, and morality in terms that are still under discussion in our culture.

The best reason for reading *Faust* is that most readers find it exciting and important. In twenty years of teaching it I have found repeatedly that students get excited about it, and the more time they have for it, the more involved they get. I have seen students use the text, legitimately, to addresses all kinds of issues. Some come to the text aware that they want to explore their own relation to Germany, the German past, or perhaps even to Nazism or the Holocaust. Others are interested in modernity and come to recognize in Faust's destructive activity the paradigmatic predicament of

7

the modern world or of the modern West. I have seen students devoted to Eastern religions become fascinated with the questions *Faust* raises about the Western theological tradition. Students of English and American literature discover the concerns of our tradition, from Hawthorne, Emerson, and Melville to James Joyce, reflected and anticipated and shaped by Goethe's play. Students and teachers disagree violently in their evaluations and interpretations of the different characters, events, and styles of writing, and the longer they have worked with the play, the more violently they disagree. There can be no doubt that *Faust* is still a provocative book.

For Germany *Faust* has been still more provocative. The Faust theme has been central to Germany's sense of identity since the mid-eighteenth century. When the critic and playwright Gotthold Ephraim Lessing proposed a specifically German tragedy in 1759, the obvious subject was Faust. In the later nineteenth century, as Germany became unified under Prussia, this literary idea took on political significance. In a short time in the 1870s Goethe's *Faust* mushroomed from being a great philosophical tragedy to being the "German Bible." Germans often described their country as the land of poets and philosophers and compared it to the philosopher-protagonist of its most famous literary work. The play was widely understood to mean that striving and action excused crimes against weaker individuals. While much in the play calls such a reading into question, it was always at hand to justify Germany's imperialist aspirations from 1870 to 1945. More humanistic and more religious reinterpretations after the war were often understood as ex post facto political exculpations. One cannot fully understand modern Germany, then, or the intellectual context of twentieth-century European politics, without some understanding of Goethe's play. The political and social implications of this text extend, through modern Europe, to our own sense of ourselves in the world.

Finally, we also live today in the shadow of the issues raised by the romantics: the problems of secularization are still with us. We worry a good deal in our culture about the role of bias in our understanding of situations, in our relations with other people, in our country's relations with other nations. We also worry about it when we frame scientific experiments, for scientists have come to realize that the way a question is asked can predetermine the answer. This is true not only for questionnaires but also for hypotheses in the hard sciences. Bias is, of course, what the romantics called subjectivity: the question of whether truth is located in subjective perception or in some transcendent object lies behind today's discussions both of cultural relativism and personal values in a diverse society, and of valid scientific method. Moral action depends on a belief that at some level there is a clear distinction between right and wrong. But when all beliefs are suspect as subjective projections of the individual, clear distinction is inaccessible to the subject, and moral or right action becomes almost impossible. *Faust*, as we will see, explores the tragic immorality of all human action because it is necessarily guided by subjective perceptions. Further, it identifies how our own ambitions to make constructive use of our knowledge drive us unwittingly to ever more destructive acts. Writing at the beginning of the modern age, Goethe delineated and addressed the fundamental issues of modernity in this text.

3

Critical Reception

Since the publication of *Faust: Part I* in 1808 critical reaction to the play has been remarkably ambivalent for a text of such stature. It has been seen as powerful but flawed, as a masterpiece but immoral, as the great work in the Faust tradition but wrong in saving its hero, as the representative work of the renascent German literature but hostile to German values. Sometimes these opposing views have been held by the same critic, especially in the earlier responses. Furthermore, because Germany was only emerging in the nineteenth century as a coherent nation-state, *Faust* was caught up in questions of national identity and became the bearer of national aspirations. This situation both explains and complicates the ambivalent reactions to *Faust* in and outside of Germany, for statements about the play became statements about Germany and German ideology. As a result the useful periods for considering the reception of *Faust* coincide increasingly with historical periods: Goethe's lifetime, the period from Goethe's death until the establishment of the German Empire (ca. 1870), the period from the Empire through World War II, and the period since the war. The history of the reception of *Faust* is to a large extent the history of Germany's view of itself in the last two centuries.

Goethe himself left enough commentary on *Faust*, in the form of letters, conversations, schemas, and variants, to support quite a range of interpretations. Such material should be used cautiously, for three reasons. The first is that Goethe worked on *Faust* for almost 60 years, from 1773 to 1832, and his ideas for the play inevitably developed and occasionally changed over that long span of time. Scholars still disagree on whether the play should be read as a unified work or as disparate segments, even though Goethe's decision to publish all of the material under the title *Faust* implies that the various parts of the play belong together. It is also clear from the documents we possess that Goethe had conceived the main outlines of the second part as he was finishing the first, even though there were considerable changes in execution 30 years later. Nevertheless, Goethe's references to *Faust* extend over the same six decades, and they necessarily seem chaotic unless a particular statement is carefully weighed against the state of the play at that moment.

The second and third reasons are of different nature but even more important. They are Goethe's love of mystification and his resistance to abstraction. He once wrote to Schiller that he would discontinue work on his novel *Wilhelm Meister* immediately if he thought that any of his readers could guess what would happen on the next page. Another time he asked Schiller to circulate several alternative interpretations of his "Fairy Tale," and in his autobiography he reports numerous episodes involving ludicrous disguises. He also had what he called a "realist tic," a tendency to avoid expressing himself explicitly. Unlike his friend Schiller, he never thought of himself as a philosopher and always tended to formulate his ideas in terms of images rather than abstractions. He preferred forms or patterns to ideas, and life and its transformations to rigid schemas. Thus he once said *Faust* had no central idea, by which he meant it could be reduced to no single, simple thematic statement, not that it lacked an organizing pattern by which it could be interpreted. His delight in mystery and his resistance to abstraction made him reticent to discuss the meaning of *Faust* and should make us wary of taking any single statement he made about it too seriously.

Goethe began *Faust* in the early 1770s, and his friends responded ecstatically—"I have a heap of [Goethe's] fragments, among others of a 'Dr. Faustus,' with some just extraordinarily splendid scenes," reports one in 1774.[2] When Goethe read from his manuscript to the Weimar court in 1780, one of the Duchess's ladies in waiting, Luise von Göchhausen, made a copy of it, which surfaced in 1887, almost a century after Goethe had destroyed his own copy. The boldness and intensity of this version, known as the *Urfaust*, made it the preferred version of the play for many scholars in the first half of this century and for some even today.

Faust only became known to a larger public when Goethe published most of the *Urfaust*, plus a few scenes that he had written in Italy, as *Faust: A Fragment* in 1790, as part of his collected works. Goethe's style had changed substantially, and his newer works did not evoke the same enthusiasm as had *The Sorrows of Young Werther*, although they are now all considered classics. Furthermore, Goethe left out the climactic scene, presumably to make clear that the text was fragmentary. *Faust* evoked little popular interest, especially since Goethe was presumed to have lost interest in it. Nevertheless, a small circle of critics and philosophers—Schiller, the Schlegel brothers, Schelling, Hegel—were so deeply touched by the *Fragment* that they ranked it with *Hamlet* and *The Divine Comedy*. Indeed, it seems to underlie their various definitions of modern philosophical tragedy.

At Schiller's prodding Goethe took up the manuscript again in 1797—with some ambivalence, as his letters show. He wrote most of the main additions to the *Fragment* by 1800, in the midst of the discussions of philosophical tragedy being conducted in Jena. Completion dragged on until 1806, the year after Schiller died. Because of the war, Part I appeared only in 1808, so that the play was again published almost 10 years after most of it was written. Goethe was now no longer the promising genius of the new literature but the grand seigneur of a flowering tradition, 59 years old and starting to seem like the survivor of an earlier generation. *Faust* was recognized as the masterpiece it had been expected to be, but was treated as if it belonged to an earlier period: it was greeted with respect, even with awe, but not with jubilation. It was 20 years before Part I was staged at all, 50 years before it was staged uncut.

The play evoked some perplexity in a generation that was turning away from the philosophical optimism of the 1790s and its drive toward universal synthesis. By this time the group of idealist philosophers in Jena had dispersed; they and their disciples continued to see the work as a monument, indeed enshrined it as an allegory of the quest for harmony between the absolute and the individual. German liberals of the 1820s and 1830s objected to this reading, and most of them to the play itself, as solipsistic, reactionary, and allegorical. There were also objections in religious quarters to the play's secularism (Coleridge refused to translate it on moral grounds), but the younger generation of romantics in France and England admired the play. Madame de Staël's *On Germany* (1810), the book that popularized German literature in France and England, propagated a simplified misreading of the play that prevailed widely in the nineteenth century. For Madame de Staël, in this "astonishing work there is no point looking for taste, control, or the art of selection and limitation; but if the mind could ever imagine an intellectual chaos like the material ones others have often described, Goethe's *Faust* would have to have been composed in such an epoch. It is not possible to surpass it in intellectual audacity, and the memory of this work always leaves a slight sense of vertigo."[3] She and her contemporaries tended to see the devil as the hero of the play, Faust as a debauchee tired of existence, and Gretchen, the girl he seduces, as an angel soiled by Faust's mindless boredom. So different is this from Goethe's play that there was a controversy in the 1830s over how to play the role of the devil; the actor who had been schooled in the role by Goethe himself in 1829 was not diabolical enough to suit his audience.

For many years it seemed that Goethe was finished with *Faust.* In 1816 he made a sketch of the second part for his autobiography specifically because he did not expect to finish it. In 1825, however, as he was preparing what he knew would be his final edition of his works, he returned to *Faust* and completed it, making the final revisions two months before his death. He refused to release the manuscript for publication until after his death, and wrote to his old friend Wilhelm von Humboldt just five days before he died, "It would unquestionably give me boundless pleasure to dedicate, share, and hear the response of my . . . friends to these very serious jokes during my lifetime. But the times are really so absurd and confused that I am convinced my long and sincere efforts on this odd structure would be ill rewarded, and lie in ruins like a wreck washed up on the beach and soon be buried in the debris-dunes of time" (17 March 1832). And Goethe's assessment was mostly correct: Part II met with general incomprehension for most of a century, and only after World War II did readers, scholars, and audiences begin to appreciate its richness and complexity.

Goethe had dominated German letters for so long that there was some sense of relief when he died. It would be wrong to say that his reputation went into eclipse, but Schiller's plays were generally more popular and less controversial. Two kinds of objections to Goethe and his work were widespread. Liberals objected to him on political grounds. Goethe had been a conservative, a supporter of monarchy and restoration, pan-European in his allegiance, while in Germany the desire for democracy and for a German nation-state went hand in hand. But conservatives also objected to him, this time on moral grounds. By the standards even of the fairly liberal 1790s, and of course by those of the Victorian nineteenth century, much of Goethe's writing was scandalous, dealing openly as it did with erotic love, seduction, adultery, divorce. *Faust* in particular raises moral issues of such complexity that they could not be dealt with in the simple black-and-white terms generally preferred by nineteenth-century culture. Goethe was resented by both Protestant and Catholic establishments. For the hundredth anniversary of his birth, efforts were made by Liszt and Wagner, among others, to establish a Goethe Society; they foundered, although a Shakespeare Society was established with great fanfare in 1864. Only two decades later, under remarkable new circumstances, did the German Goethe Society come into being. Nevertheless, important voices continued to speak for him—Heine, Stifter, Engels in Germany, George Eliot in England—and the bases for the voluminous scholarship on his life and reading were laid by Heinrich Düntzer.

Faust became more than ever *the* German figure during this period after Goethe's death, but the Faust whom people had in mind in their frequent references was much more like the hero of Christopher Marlowe's *Dr. Faustus*, whose pact with the devil was unmistakably evil and who was carried off to hell. He was also much more rooted in the German sixteenth century than was Goethe's figure, who transcends all cultures and times. Goethe was often criticized for not making his Faust more German and for allowing his hero to escape the devil. The many plays and operas that were written in response to Goethe's *Faust*—by Lenau, Grabbe, Berlioz, Gounod, and Gilbert, to name but a few—imitate the kind of *Faust* described by popularizers like Madame de Staël and are more Byronic than Goethean. It is hard to imagine a masterpiece as widely recognized yet as misunderstood.

Attitudes toward Goethe changed rapidly in the late 1860s. As Bismarck extended the power of Prussia, German liberals gave up their hopes for a republic in exchange for a unified Germany, and the Second Empire was declared. This new German Empire immediately adopted Goethe as its cultural father figure. When Goethe's grandchildren left the poet's papers to the grand duchess of Weimar, there were no objections to establishing not only a Goethe Society (1885) but also an archive and a critical edition of his works. His classical plays (*Iphigenia, Egmont, Tasso*) and the idyll *Hermann and Dorothea* became required reading in schools, and there was a tremendous explosion of research and scholarship on Goethe's life and the backgrounds and meaning of his works (some 6,000 publications on him had appeared by the end of the century). Goethe was now deified as "the Olympian," representative of the highest ideals of the European tradition. The power of this image at the turn of the century is reflected in the work of the founding fathers of psychoanalysis. Freud writes about his adolescent compulsion to read every word in Goethe's complete works, while Jung begins his autobiography by denying the "rumor" that he is an illegitimate grandson of the great poet. In some sense all German intellectuals of the period (and a great many outside Germany) are illegitimate grandsons of Goethe.

During this period of Goethe idolatry Faust became more than ever the paradigm of the German nation. In the heyday of the German Empire *Faust* was spoken of as "the second German Bible," and in Oswald Spengler's *Decline of the West* (1918) Goethe's hero symbolizes the entirety of Western culture. Faust's pact with the devil was understood not as evil but as good; his restlessness, his drive to achieve and build at all costs, were the ideal of Western civilization. That Goethe ultimately saved Faust was seen as the stamp of approval for German (and European) expansionism in the crassest sense. Every side in the political debate used Goethe. Soldiers marched off to World War I with *Faust* in their knapsacks, but between the wars the short-lived German republic located its capital in Weimar—Goethe's city—in an effort to renounce Prussian militarism. Yet when the Nazis moved the capital back to Berlin, they took *Faust* along, and carried it off to World War II in their knapsacks as well. This ideological abuse of the text depended on a version different from Madame de Staël's, but also on one equally limited and distorted, and one that still had more to do with the sixteenth-century Faust than with Goethe's. So extreme was the distortion of the text that a series of efforts began in the early 1930s by more liberal-minded Germans (scholars like Wilhelm Böhm, authors like Thomas Mann) to separate Goethe from the Faust tradition and to reestablish him as a European. They were mostly ignored until after World War II.

Since the war there have been important adjustments in the understanding of *Faust*, but the intensive political exploitation of the text and its author since the 1870s has left an ambivalence even more profound than that which greeted the work's first appearance. In some respects the tradition of Goethe idolatry, the perception of Goethe as father figure, and the old interpretations of the play have persisted. The basic tools of Goethe scholarship, especially commentaries of *Faust*, date originally from the turn of the century. While adjustments have certainly been made in new editions and in newly written commentaries, a remarkable proportion of the older interpretation has survived intact in current school editions in Germany. At a more obvious level, the cultural propaganda arm of the German government is officially named the Goethe Institute.

Not surprisingly, the generation that came of age in the 1960s, as it tried to free itself from the burden of the Nazi past, needed to free itself from Goethe as well. Goethe was attacked from various ideological viewpoints, criticized on aesthetic grounds, and staged in productions that undermined the values that the texts had always been understood to represent. It is hard to imagine the intensity and virulence of such attacks in America, where art has rarely achieved the public significance and ideological engagement it still has in most European cultures. It is not uncommon, for example, to produce modern—sometimes quite shocking—productions of, say, Shakespeare in this country. But such productions normally confront the audience with its own limitations in the face of Shakespeare's universality. Equivalent productions of Goethe's work in Germany in the last 30 years or so have, to be sure, confronted their audiences with their own limitations, but have also implied that their limitations are Goethe's as well. To admire Goethe in Germany has ideological implications.

Within the context of Goethe scholarship this ambivalence has been reflected in two important ways. The first has been the rediscovery of Part II. In the 1950s and early 1960s there appeared major scholarly works on Part II that defined a new Goethe who had more in common with the Goethe of Thomas Mann and Wilhelm Böhm. Critics who discussed Part II at all had tended to focus on the first scene and on act 5; now careful reading and explication of the first four acts revealed that they were not the products of senility, hopelessly esoteric, or utterly indifferent to Goethe's political and social milieu—all of which had been asserted. As we have learned to read Goethe's late works, we have found there a Goethe who cared passionately about integrating German culture into the European tradition and about anchoring modern society in its past before that past became entirely unrecognizable—a Goethe who was remarkably prescient about the implications of the technological revolution for human society.

The second aspect of the ambivalence about Goethe appears in a widespread disagreement about how to understand the ending of the play, in which Faust is carried off to heaven. So-called perfectibilists understand the end to be meant seriously—that is, that Faust truly is saved and that his mode of being is in some sense affirmed. This reading was already articulated by a few of the more prescient readers of the *Fragment* of 1790 and has prevailed ever since. It has become, however, ideologically suspect because a crass version of it was politically abused for so long. The opposing position that has emerged with increasing strength in recent years asserts that the end is ironic, even bitter, and that Faust's mode of being throughout the play is condemned. Substantial and thoughtful arguments have been made for both positions by scholars with various degrees of commitment to different ideological stances in and outside of Germany. Indeed, it is clear that the play was intended to raise questions and provoke controversy. The ambivalence that has surrounded the play responds to questions urgently asked, but not explicitly answered in the play itself. Its complexity has allowed successive ages to read *Faust* in terms of their own deepest concerns.

A Reading

¶

4

Goethe and the Faust Tradition

There is a long tradition of stories and plays about the scholar who makes a pact with the devil, a tale that dates back to early Christian times. In the late nineteenth century scholars collected all of these versions and established the so-called Faust tradition. While it is often helpful to consider such material in order to appreciate particular details in *Faust*, it is important to use these texts thoughtfully, for two reasons. First, Goethe did not necessarily know all of these works. The most important of them, for example, Christopher Marlowe's *The Tragical History of Dr. Faustus*, was probably unknown to Goethe except by title until he read a translation of it in 1818, 10 years after Part I had been published. Second, Goethe diverges from the tradition as often as he follows it. The most important and famous example of this is that his Faust is not damned. Instead, Goethe consistently undermines the ethics of all previous treatments of the Faust legend. It is generally best to use the Faust tradition as a standard against which to recognize just what is interesting and unusual about Goethe's text.

The Faust legend per se begins in the sixteenth century, when the story of the scholar who promises his soul to the devil in return for knowledge, power, or a beautiful woman becomes attached to a historical person named Georg Faust (ca. 1480–ca. 1540), a charlatan notorious for his interest in astrology, alchemy, and medicine.

In 1587 an anonymous chapbook (an inexpensive pamphlet for popular consumption) described his pact and subsequent adventures with the devil, laced with comic and satiric anecdotes of all sorts and ending with Faust's destruction and damnation. The book appears to have been written by a Protestant pastor partly as an attack on Catholicism (this is the century of the Protestant Reformation) and partly as an attack on Renaissance humanism. This latter attack, however, is ambivalent, for the narrator of the book is himself learned and seems to share, at least in part, the humanists' admiration for classical antiquity. He presents Faust as a negative example, a sinner of the worst sort, yet still a figure who compels our interest if not quite our sympathy. The book was extremely popular, with a second edition and English translation following almost immediately. A substantially enlarged elaboration appeared in 1599; another one, with further additions in 1674; and yet another, greatly revised, version in 1725. The story was still sold in an inexpensive pamphlet at fairs during Goethe's childhood, by which time Faust was established as a permanent type in the German cultural consciousness.

Christopher Marlowe's *The Tragical History of Dr. Faustus* (ca. 1590), today the best-known Elizabethan play apart from any by Shakespeare, was based closely on the English translation of the original German chapbook of 1587. It is the greatest of the literary treatments of the legend before Goethe's. Its hero's concern for power is typical of Elizabethan tragedy, and the way Marlowe intensifies the chapbook's ambivalent treatment of Faust makes him a tragic hero whose fate seems deserved but who still evokes our sympathy. Marlowe includes not only the details of Faust's pact with Mephistopheles and his subsequent damnation but also some of the comic anecdotes and anti-Catholic satire from the chapbook—so much, in fact, that some scholars have argued that an interpolator defaced Marlowe's pure tragedy. There is, however, no compelling evidence for such a theory, and we must assume that Marlowe was comfortable with the comic material in the chapbook.

Marlowe's play returned to Germany with English troupes of actors who performed there in the late sixteenth and early seventeenth centuries. Such English comedians, as they were known, performed plays from the London stage, first in English, then in rather limited German adaptations. Later their plays passed into local hands and were performed in still-shorter and more distorted versions, even as puppet plays. This is the form in which Goethe probably first encountered Faust. It seems likely that these popular productions placed increasingly heavy emphasis on the comic aspects of the play and imported comedy into the more serious parts as well, including the relationship between Faust and Mephistopheles.

It may seem odd to us, with our strict notions of the difference between comedy and tragedy, that Marlowe's play could degenerate into low comedy—and even odder that a great writer like Goethe should continue this tradition, which he indubitably did. If we look, however, at other magician figures in Renaissance literature, we see that a tragic magician was the exception, not the rule. In Elizabethan drama the most famous magician besides Marlowe's is Prospero in Shakespeare's *Tempest*. Like Faust's, Prospero's magical powers are mostly used for trickery of various sorts, and Prospero knows that magic is evil. He finally renounces magic, but only after he has punished his enemies and recovered his ducal power. He is, in effect, a Faust in a play in which evil is less powerful and events end happily. This pattern is much more common for Renaissance magicians than Marlowe's pattern, as Goethe well knew; in act 1 of Part II he draws an explicit parallel between his own Faust and Shakespeare's Prospero. Thus, it is not surprising that Faust turns up as the subject of puppet plays, comedies, and ballets in the seventeenth and eighteenth centuries.

In 1759 Gotthold Ephraim Lessing, the leading playwright and critic in Germany at the time, proposed a Faust tragedy as the obvious example of the kind of play that would be a German masterpiece. In this famous polemical statement, in the essay "Seventeenth Letter on Literature," Lessing encouraged German dramatists to do something other than simply translate or imitate what was being written in France and to a lesser extent in England. He offered Faust as a specifically German theme, since he was the only popular literary figure of German origin. Lessing suggested tragedy (rather than comedy) because he operated within a critical system—the dominant one in the period—that identified tragedy as the highest form of serious literature.

Goethe had been brought up in the same critical system as Lessing, and furthermore admired him greatly; thus, it was almost a given that he should intend his Faust play to be a tragedy. However, he was in the process of abjuring that system, neoclassicism, when he began work on *Faust*. For reasons that perhaps no one understands, Goethe was unusually tolerant of mixing comedy and tragedy, of including elements of opera, pageantry, and the popular stage in formal drama; he was also unusually open to learning about and testing literary styles from other cultures, even by the rather liberal standards of the romantic period. He continued to call *Faust* a tragedy but admitted into it all kinds of elements that can be found in no other tragedy. It is thus particularly important to keep in mind that the Faust tradition itself is not always tragic, and above all not to allow standard definitions of tragedy or memories of Marlowe's play to interfere with what Goethe wrote.

The kind of drama *Faust* turned out to be is called world theater. It represents human action in relation to the divine cosmos rather than only in relation to human society. Often in such plays God and the devil appear as characters on stage; often other figures who are obviously not "real," like Lust or Jealousy, appear as well. Central to such drama is that it represents not what is real in the ordinary sense but higher truth. For this reason the audience does not expect to be taken in by the illusions on stage; it expects instead to be instructed by what it knows are representations of what cannot be seen, of what has never physically existed. Passion plays, morality plays, court masques, Spanish Corpus Christi plays (popular through the seventeenth century), and many operas belong in this category.

One of the great achievements of Marlowe's *Dr. Faustus* is that it starts to move English drama out of this mode and into the one more familiar to us, in which characters seem psychologically real, and we focus more on the inner development of characters than on their relation to the larger context. Goethe reverses Marlowe's achievement when he writes *Faust*, partly because he wants to explore the relation of the self to the larger cosmos. But the late eighteenth century no longer believed in God and the devil with the same confidence as the sixteenth and seventeenth centuries, so Goethe's world theater looks quite different from that of the Renaissance. It explores, as we shall see, the ways in which literature represents the world with this mode. *Faust* has at its disposal all the techniques of the tragic tradition of the inner self that Marlowe helped found, yet also consciously recalls a theater that locates the self in a larger context. Thus, Goethe's play differs fundamentally from all earlier treatments of the Faust legend. Goethe changed not only *what* the Faust legend represents, but also *how* it represents.

5

Formulating the Problems

Faust is a very long and very confusing play. For this reason it is especially important to know what questions an interpretation should pose, and what kind of statements would answer them. Only then can we judge our success, or even know when to stop. This chapter will be devoted, therefore, to defining the goals of interpretation for *Faust*.

We have interpreted a text when we have found a language that enables us to describe it and its patterns of ideas, style, imagery, and allusions coherently, in terms that also apply to other literary, philosophical, or visual works of its period and of other periods. All interpretation must start by choosing its target language. We could, for example, agree that we have interpreted the text when we have explained the motivations of its characters and/or of its author in terms of their repressed childhood experiences. Depending on whose terminology we adopt to describe such patterns in the play, we would arrive at a psychoanalytic interpretation—perhaps Freudian, perhaps Jungian. Or we could decide that we have understood the text when we have traced in it the impact of particular historical circumstances—say, economic, political, or philosophical. Whatever questions we ask can be answered well or badly, so that there can be good and bad interpretations; but without the questions of the interpreter, there can be no interpretation. When I described the philosophical concerns of romanticism in chapter 1, which addresses the historical context of *Faust*, I defined the language in which we will agree that we have arrived at a coherent description of the text.

We also need a text to have an interpretation. With a play as long and as complicated as *Faust* it would be naive to think that we could interpret every line or scene with equal care and do full justice to the text as it really is. In fairness to the reader, then, a brief plot summary of the play as I read it appears in the Appendix. This summary may also help to orient readers who have read only excerpts from the play, because the discussion below will not always follow the sequence of the plot.

In order to formulate the problems to be addressed in *Faust*, let us consider the three prologues (*Dedication, Prelude in the Theater, Prologue in Heaven*) and a few pages of the first scene in which Faust is on stage (*Night*), and then ask what needs to be explained and what aspects of the play make it difficult and/or interesting to read.

Notice first that there are three prologues—why was one not enough? A preliminary answer emerges immediately: the three are very different from one another. In *Dedication* the poet speaks to us in his own melancholy voice about his hesitation to resume work on the play. The *Prelude*, by contrast, is a lively, even rambunctious discussion among a director, poet, and harlequin about the play they want to stage. The poet sounds, to be sure, rather like the poet who speaks in *Dedication*, but he is now only one voice in three, and the harlequin, not he, seems to speak with the most authority. The *Prologue in Heaven* shifts away from comedy with its elevated hymn of the three archangels (Where did they come from? What have they to do with the conversation we just overheard?), and shifts the tone back again with the argument between the Lord and Mephistopheles, which sounds a little like the one we just heard between the director, poet, and harlequin. As we continue into the beginning of *Night* we are immediately struck by the constant shifts in Faust's mood—a student of mine once described him as manic-depressive—as he alternates between despair and ecstatic contemplation of nature. These differences reveal amazing instability in the point of view; tone, mood, location, subject matter can change abruptly from one scene to the next, even from one line to the next. These prologues establish the pattern that change is important and that it can be abrupt.

It is particularly difficult to pin the characters down. In *Dedication* the speaker seems to be Goethe himself speaking about *Faust*. But when a similar voice, labeled simply "poet," speaks in the *Prelude*, we realize that perhaps the speaker in *Dedication* is any poet, not just Goethe. In the *Prelude* the harlequin mediates between the director and the poet; in the *Prologue in Heaven* there is still a harlequin figure, but now he has a name, Mephistopheles (in one of the most successful productions of *Faust* in this century, both roles are played by the same actor, who is already made up as the devil when he appears in the *Prelude*). Are we to understand that the harlequin of the *Prelude* was already really the devil? or that the devil is only a harlequin and not to be taken seriously? That point of view and perhaps even identity can change shows that we can never be too confident about what we know—about the play and, by implication, about the world. The problem of point of view, or perspective, and its relation to knowledge will be central in our reading of *Faust*.

We have, however, already noticed some continuities: the voice of the poet connects *Dedication* and the *Prelude*; the voice of the harlequin connects the *Prelude* and the *Prologue*. What else? Suppose we ask "What happens?" or "What is supposed to happen?" in each. In *Dedication* the poet wants to write a poem that he had long left untouched; to do so he must recover his mood of years before and regain contact with his past. In the *Prelude* all three characters want to create a play. To do so, however, the harlequin must reconcile the disparate views of the director, who cares only about what his worldly public wants, with those of the poet, who cares only about his unworldly ideals. In the *Prologue* we see the Lord and Mephistopheles enter into a wager about how Faust will behave when the devil tempts him. In a sense they are planning another play—one in which the director, Mephistopheles, will not be able to control his hero, but a play nevertheless. (Notice how Mephistopheles' role has already shifted from harlequin to director; this is typical of *Faust* and its shifting perspectives). All three prologues involve the creation of a text or performance, which in each case mediates between oppositions—between the poet's present and his own past, between the worldliness of the director and the idealism of the poet, between the optimism of the Lord and the cynicism of Mephistopheles with regard to the human race. Such reconciliation of opposites constitutes a series of dialectics in the first chapter, and here we see the centrality of the dialectical structure for *Faust*.

If each of the prologues is organized in terms of a dialectic, we must ask after the relation among them. All move toward creating a play, but the audiences for them vary greatly. In *Dedication* the poet's visions rise before his own eyes, in the *Prelude* they play to a typical eighteenth-century public, in the *Prologue in Heaven* Faust will be observed by God and the devil—the moral cosmos. We might characterize the three prologues by saying that *Dedication* shows us an individual version, the *Prelude* a social version, and the *Prologue* a religious version of the same process. Clearly, there is a progression that will help us define the forms of the dialectic to look for in *Faust*.

The exact course of the dialectic in *Dedication* is difficult to trace. The main opposition is between past and present: the speaker feels assaulted by the old fragments of his text (first stanza), then alternately pleased and grieved by the memories of old friends, most now gone forever. Finally, inspiration gently seizes him in the last stanza and brings his memories to life. It is unclear whether memory causes inspiration or whether poetic inspiration makes memory more acceptable, but it does not seem to matter. For the speaker, poetic inspiration and memory both temporarily bridge the unhappy gap between present and past. And this sets a pattern: in the *Prelude*, after the harlequin formulates a compromise between the director and the poet, the poet responds,

> Then give me the times again,
> When I myself was still growing,
> When a bursting fountain of song
> Constantly renewed itself . . .
> Give me back my youth! (184–97)

Similarly, in *Night* Faust decides not to commit suicide because the Easter chorus he overhears from the neighboring church awakens memories of childhood (769–84). Over and over in Part I memory is associated with states of calm and connection to a truth difficult to access. Faust speaks of happy memories when he first visits Margarete's room and again in his first speech in *Forest and Cavern*, his moment of greatest satisfaction in Part I. In Part II Faust enters bodily into the realm of memory when he goes to the

Classical Walpurgis Night and encounters figures from Greek mythology and eventually marries Helen of Troy. As memory extends from the personal to the collective past, Goethe questions the implications of historicism and uses dialectical structures to confront the uniqueness of history with its simultaneous repetitiveness.

The *Prelude* offers a dialectic concerned with art. The director seeks to please his public only with sensual stimuli, not with the integrity or significance of the work of art. Thus, he makes little distinction between drama and food as forms of public entertainment and is eager to serve his play as a mixture of pieces, like a tasty stew (99-100). His point of view offends the poet, who rejects the public's right to entertainment. He yearns rather for the "silent narrow gate of Heaven" (63), for the "magnificent chords" (149) of divine harmony, for eternal truth, and his vocabulary is consistently religious in tone. The harlequin keeps the two together by suggesting that their play be a love story, which is varied enough for the director yet coherent enough for the poet. In this opposition between worldliness and higher truth we see the outlines of the dialectic of world and spirit reconciled by love, which the eighteenth century had inherited from Renaissance neoplatonism.

The dialectic is, however, modified in a characteristic and important way. As we have already seen, the reconciled poet invokes the power of memory as he decides to continue his work with the director. And as in *Dedication* this moment is also associated with poetry, for the harlequin has recommended not love itself but a play about love. We will talk more about this self-consciousness later. Here we will register only that Goethe typically has world and spirit come together in art, so that *Faust* will be in great part a play about art, its function, and its limits.

The *Prologue in Heaven*, the play promised in the *Prelude*, continues this concern at another level. God and Mephistopheles represent by definition the opposition between spirit and world; they are connected by their common interest in (love for?) man. They both talk about man in the future tense: God anticipates that he will always ultimately mean well, even as he makes mistakes, while Mephistopheles sees only how he will fail. They articulate not facts but potentials, and thus they embody opposing perspectives on what man can be, rather than opposing principles of good and evil. Similarly, in his tolerance God sees both nature and the passage of time as orderly: he compares man to a tree that will grow and bear fruit. For the cynical Mephistopheles, by contrast, nature and time are meaningless and repetitive: man is like a grasshopper, leaping up and always falling back. Even the dialectic can be a matter of point of view in this play.

But if the ultimate value of existence depends on point of view, then how are we, as spectators, to know whether God or the devil is right? We have a built-in bias toward God, but the version of God on stage does not inspire the awe and terror of the God of the Old Testament. Goethe's eminently civil and tolerant elderly gentleman mocked by a witty devil has left many readers uncomfortable with divine authority in the play. If even God's opinion is not dependably valid, there is a serious problem with our ability to know anything. This epistemological uncertainty moves us into the realm of the romantic dialectic of the knowing subject and the object of knowledge.

In fact, the hymn of the archangels, which precedes the discussion between God and Mephistopheles, has already introduced this problem. The angels sing in praise of nature, which for them represents the glory of God. The archangels especially celebrate its incomprehensibility, remarking on it three times within four lines (248–51) and again in their final chorus. God is also often unknowable in the Old Testament, whose language Goethe borrows here; He is especially unknowable in the Book of Job, from which the exchange between God and the devil comes. Raphael introduces the theme in the first stanza:

> The sight [of the sun] gives the angels strength,
> Though none can fathom it;
> The incomprehensibly great works
> Are splendid as on the first day. (247–50)

All three archangels repeat the theme at the end of the hymn:

> The sight gives the angels strength,
> Since none can fathom Thee;
> And all Thy great works
> Are splendid as on the first day. (267–70)

The incomprehensibility of the creation becomes the incomprehensibility of God, and it frames their entire hymn. If God is unfathomable to the archangels, how much more so is He to us, and to Faust, whom He never addresses directly. God in this play is as unknowable as the Kantian object.

If God is unknowable, how can we see Him, and why is He such an unassuming, perhaps even unimpressive, old gentleman? Some directors have avoided the issue by representing God with a disembodied voice. Of course we cannot see God, but we can see an actor who represents Him. We already know that God is an actor in *Faust* because the *Prelude in the Theater* has made the *Prologue* a play-within-the-play. If God looks unspectacular to us, that reminds us that the figure on stage is not God at all but only a representation, and a particularly stagy one at that. The unknowable object is visible to us only in play. Much of *Faust* consists of plays staged within the play. From the love scenes with Margarete to the marriage to Helena to Faust's ultimate flood-control projects, these plays are Faust's moments of highest insight and achievement.

But who can write such plays? How can the poet of the *Prelude*, or Faust and Mephistopheles, the most frequent authors in the play, have access to invisible truth? If, in the terms of the romantic dialectic, the subject renders the invisible object visible by fashioning a representation of it, in what sense does the play truly represent the object itself and not merely the subject's own projection? We will see increasingly sophisticated efforts to validate the representations of transcendent truth in the plays-within-the-play.

So far we have discussed tone, style, and structure. The wager between God and Mephistopheles also raises moral questions. The fanciful nature of the first two prologues has no impact on what happens in the play, but the bet between the Lord and the devil in the *Prologue in Heaven* does affect Faust's later pact with the devil, the very heart of the Faust story. God's argument turns on the lines "Man errs as long as he strives" (317) and "A good man in his dark urge / Is still conscious of the right path" (328–29). These are generalizations about human nature, not statements about Faust alone. We have already seen how the Lord and the devil articulate attitudes toward man, so that the issue is really the vocation of man (the latter phrase is the title, by the way, of one of the best-known treatises written in response to Kant by J. G. Fichte). The Lord and Mephistopheles agree to test Faust, but how seriously this test is to be taken is another problem. Even God says that Faust's behavior is not that expected from a beloved servant: "Even if he serves me with confusion now, / I shall soon lead him into clarity" (308-9). Later he adds, "Man errs as long as he strives" (317). If man always errs, resisting the devil is not what leads to salvation. Apparently the vocation of man in *Faust* is not to be good in the traditional sense but to strive.

How can Goethe have meant this? In his striving in Part I Faust will murder two people and abandon his mistress to execution for infanticide. In Part II his striving will lead him into dubious political schemes, economic swindles, selfish exploitation of war, and further murder of innocents. How can striving in itself be good, as many late-nineteenth- and twentieth-century readers of the play believed? Clearly, the play shows us it cannot, and indeed, the *Prologue* makes no such claim. Striving, we are told, is the vocation of man; it is "natural" to man. As long as an individual fulfills his human nature by striving, God can take an interest in him and lead him "into clarity," despite the errors he will inevitably have made. The issue here is what it means to be human, not the battle between good and evil. Thus, the Lord can say that he has never hated Mephistopheles, because his temptations keep man from being lazy. In this context the devil is simply a "companion, / Who pricks and works and must act as devil" (342-43). The devil is not, in this formulation, a principle of evil, nor is God a principle of good. They are the names of necessary oppositions in the order of nature, like birth and death.

If the order of the cosmos subsumes both good and evil, morality is much more of a problem than it is in a world where evil has its proper place. Goethe confronts us in *Faust* with a morally indifferent natural order within which Faust must attempt to live as a civilized moral being. But if nature is not moral, man cannot both fulfill his natural vocation to strive and still live morally. This is the moral version of the romantic dilemma, of the categorical separation between self and world. And this is what makes *Faust* a tragedy.

We have raised several issues that will be important for understanding *Faust*; let us summarize them here. Four issues arose from the way the play is written—the instability of the point of view, dialectical structures, the importance of play-within-the-play, the thoroughgoing staginess of the play. We also raised five thematic issues—change, the three major dialectics (present versus past, world versus spirit, subject versus object), art as the resolution of most sets of oppositions in the play, the dilemma that arises when art projected by an individual is taken as the representation of general truth, and the moral dilemma that arises from the discrepancy between the natural and the moral orders. The ease with which the discussion has moved between stylistic and thematic issues, and the necessity that it do so, are what make *Faust* a poem rather than a philosophical tract. If we tried to read it as a tract, looking only at what it says, we would miss much of what is most interesting and entertaining in the play.

6

Faust, Mephistopheles, and Their Bargain

The pact between Faust and Mephistopheles, the heart of the Faust legend, was one of the most difficult parts of the play for Goethe to write. In the 1770s he skipped it to get on with his unique contribution, the seduction of Margarete, and only in the late nineties, when he had committed himself to finishing the play, did he return to fill the gap that extended from the first half of *Night* to the appearance of the student at the end of *Study*. These scenes, commonly referred to as the "tragedy of the scholar," elaborate the problems introduced in the prologues. Since the play is often bewildering in its detail, the point here will be to clarify its underlying consistency.

THE DIALECTICS

Faust dominates the first two scenes, *Night* and *Before the City Gate*, but his mood veers between despair and euphoria. He begins in depression, rejecting the entire sixteenth-century university curriculum; no book learning, nothing that can be formulated in words satisfies him. But there is a series of emotional high points: he dreams of dancing with spirits in the moonlight (386–97), he feels in harmony with all being as he contemplates the sign of the macrocosm (430–53), he aspires to fellowship with the earth spirit

(460–511), he toasts the morning (with a chalice of poison! [686–736]), he feels at one with nature at the beginning of his Easter walk (903–40), and he dreams, finally, of joining the sun in its eternal circling in his impassioned last speech to the setting sun (1070–99). In between, he despairs at his imprisonment in his study, among books, in the academic pedantry personified by Wagner, in the limits of earthly existence, in the limits of human error. So regular is this pattern that his return to earthly limitation seems increasingly inevitable after each succeeding flight of enthusiasm.

At first the human world seems constrained, symbolized as it is by Faust's musty study, but in *Before the City Gate* the pleasant, grateful world of society on Easter morning shows that it really is the proper place for man (as Faust himself briefly realizes, [940]), and it is normal for Faust to keep returning to it, whatever his attitude. Similarly, in the moment when he seeks to transcend life by taking poison, he turns the beyond into the real world and ends up toasting death as "morning." At the end of *Before the City Gate* he finally exclaims,

> Two souls, alas, dwell within my breast
> One wants to part from the other;
> The one, in love's fierce desire, holds fast
> To the world with clinging organs;
> The other rises powerfully from the dust
> To the realms of lofty forebears. (1112–17)

Each soul desires strongly as it pulls against the other; each strives and is therefore, in the terms of the *Prologue in Heaven*, essentially human. Faust's whole self comprises both souls, or perspectives. Neither is "right" or "best," but both are natural and human. The situation is like the moral situation in the *Prologue*, in which both good and evil are part of the natural order.

Beginning in *Study*, Faust's mood swings become muted as opposition to Mephistopheles replaces opposition to himself. In their conflict Faust mostly represents the positive, idealistic view of human capabilities, and Mephistopheles the more negative, worldly view (as reflected also in his cynicism in the *Prologue in Heaven*). Faust speaks for the soul that strives for higher regions, while Mephistopheles encourages and speaks for the one that clings to the dust of earth (in his wager with the Lord, the devil hopes to drag Faust down and make him eat dust [334]). Mephistopheles thus takes over a voice that was formerly within Faust. This situation fits with God's assertion in the *Prologue* that Mephistopheles is to prick from below to prevent laziness; it will often be difficult to see how Mephistopheles is opposing rather than assisting Faust. When Mephistopheles advises the student (1868–2050) this doubleness appears in comic form. Disguised as Faust, he is a distorted, demonic parody of Faust's own wisdom and learning; at the same time, the innocent and eager young student parodies Faust's own naivete in concluding a pact with the devil. With his role divided between these two characters, Faust suddenly appears to be both more destructive and more naive than we had perhaps thought. Already part of the *Urfaust*, this scene demonstrates how deeply rooted perspectivism is in Goethe's conception of the play.

In his later years Goethe elaborated his concern with perspectives. Polarized light fascinated him, because it showed how illumination from different angles was a basic phenomenon of nature. His last novel, *Wilhelm Meister's Journeyman Years* (1829), addresses the same issues over and over from different points of view in a medley of novellas, essays, dialogues, and aphorisms. Perspectivism found its most famous formulation in an essay called "Repeated Reflections" (1823), in which Goethe collects and juxtaposes several versions of the same event in his life, showing how each new perspective enlarges our understanding. Accordingly, mirrors—and by metaphorical extension, images of all kinds—are important in his work, for every reflection extends knowledge.

Faust and Mephistopheles are the most important names for the central perspectives in *Faust*; let us now examine the structures into which they are organized by considering the different names given to the goals of Faust's striving. As he rejects word mongering (385) in his opening speech, he turns to magic "In order to learn what holds / The world together at its very center, / To see the cause and seed of all action" (382–84). Because Faust longs to understand nature, he turns to the moonlight beyond his dirty windowpanes and dreams of spirits hovering in a mountain landscape and bathing in the dew. Now knowledge is not verbal but involves immersion in its object. This development intensifies with the sign of the macrocosm, where the knowledge courses through

Faust's veins. Now nature seems divine to him, and he sees "heavenly powers" (449) ascending and descending between earth and heaven, as Jacob did in his dream (Genesis 28). As he confronts the earth spirit he sees nature less as a manifestation of divinity than as divinity itself. It is no longer an object of knowledge but a dangerous creative force that Faust claims to resemble but cannot really comprehend (compare the incomprehensibility of God in the *Prologue in Heaven*). Even the vial of poison represents nature to Faust, for he notices it with the words "Why does it suddenly seem lovely and bright, / As when moonlight wafts about us in the night-dark forest?" (688–89). Yet this poison also carries him into a traditional landscape of transcendence, a gate through which he passes into some higher life above the clouds. The Easter chorus that immediately follows shapes the episode even more into the standard religious form, for Christ was resurrected from death to a new life of the body. Finally, in Faust's speech to the sunset he longs for wings to follow the sun around the earth. He will be in the sky, on a "course like a god's" (1080), and yet in constant touch with the landscape, which he describes in loving detail. This is the same mixed landscape described by the archangels in their hymn. Combining excitement and calm, high and low, permanent evening and eternal light, it is the ultimate fusion of divine and natural, the revelation of divine order in nature.

Thus, Faust's initial longing for knowledge of nature intensifies to a longing for communion with it. At the same time nature is increasingly imbued with spiritual power and is less and less physical nature. The beginning of *Study* reiterates the spiritual goal of Faust's desire for knowledge. He sets out to translate the Gospel according to John, "In the beginning was the *logos*," usually translated "word." He balks, naturally, at the translation "word," for he had vigorously rejected "word-mongering" in his opening monologue. In quick succession he substitutes "sense," "power," and "deed," thus summarizing his stages in *Night*—for "sense" suggests the feelings evoked by the sign of the macrocosm, "power" those evoked by the earth spirit, and "deed" the rhetoric of his suicide speech. The sentence in the Gospel continues, however, "and the *logos* was with God, and the *logos* was God." In seeking unity with nature, Faust really strives to know transcendence, or what the neoplatonist tradition called spirit or mind. But as the *Prologue in*

Heaven has already made clear, such knowledge is inaccessible to the human mind. Thus, as Faust invokes divinity in ever more explicit terms in these two scenes, he is also pulled back into the physical world with increasing vigor. He is caught in the neoplatonist dialectic of world and spirit.

Such language of inaccessible knowledge immediately evokes the romantic dialectic as well. In seeking transcendence Faust strives after knowledge of what is categorically other from himself: transcendence is not only the divine One but also the Kantian object. And Faust is trapped not only in the world but also in his own study. He complains about its narrowness and refers to it repeatedly as a prison from which he longs to escape. Its Gothic architecture suggests that it represents the narrowness of the Middle Ages, whose confining curriculum Faust also seeks to escape. But because this prison is cluttered with the artifacts of his own search, it also reminds him too much of the individual self that he has found instead of the knowledge of the Other that he seeks. His final attempt at escape in *Night* is suicide: What could say more clearly that his dark study represents the confines of his own subjectivity and that what he seeks in nature outside is the object?

In these attempts to escape, Faust repeatedly defines his self in terms of his past. His cell is cluttered with the "household stuff of remote ancestors" (408); the chalice into which he pours the poison is a family heirloom. In *Before the City Gate* the memory of his and his father's efforts to cure the plague brings on one of his most bitter depressions, while the Easter chorus recalls his childhood to him and thus reconciles him to the middle course of life in nature (the experience shared by the poets in *Dedication* and the *Prelude*). If Faust needs to clarify his relationship to nature and to transcendence, he also needs to clarify his relationship to the past. He is thus also engaged in the historicist dialectic of past and present. All three of the dialectics defined in the prologues are present here, and in each Faust strives to reach what is categorically inaccessible to human comprehension.

The place now left for Mephistopheles in these dialectics seems at first unusual for a supernatural figure like the devil. At the end of *Before the City Gate* Faust longs for beneficent spirits of the air, who float between earth and heaven (the purviews of his two souls), to descend and carry him off to a new life. Mephistopheles fulfills his wish; he is the black poodle that accompanies Faust home to his study, and he will shortly whisk him away on a magic carpet. It first appears, then, that Mephistopheles will mediate between Faust's two souls, and he often does so in the rest of the play.

Nevertheless, he also frequently speaks for the soul that clings to the world, as we have already seen. In almost every other version of the Faust legend Faust conjures the devil with elaborate incantations and ceremonies, and it is hard to imagine a less dramatic way to introduce the devil than Goethe has chosen. Back in Faust's study the dog begins to grow, so that Faust compares it first to a hippopotamus (1254), then to an elephant (1311), all the while trying to exorcise it with charms against the spirits of the four elements. Although Mephistopheles lacks a stable form, all his forms remain within the animal world, and Faust assumes he must be a nature spirit. Furthermore, his only visible henchmen in these scenes are also animals, like the rats who set him free, or nature spirits. Later Mephistopheles will appear as a wandering scholar, later still (and most commonly) as a baron, but never as the red monster with horns, tail, and pitchfork. Mephistopheles is consistently tied to the natural world.

Being natural, he is enmeshed in the dialectical structure of the cosmos, as Faust is. He calls himself "A part of that power, / That always wills evil, and always achieves good" (1335-36). Look at what happens to him when he tries to explain his place as negator: "I am a part of the part, that in the beginning was all, / A part of the darkness that gave birth to light, / The proud light that now denies Mother Night / Her old precedence, her space" (1349-52). No sooner does Mephistopheles explain his origins than they give birth to their opposite—here, dark to light. This principle of destruction can talk about his background only in terms of birth and is immediately seen by Faust as the "son" of chaos (1384). Mephistopheles admits, furthermore, to a complete inability to destroy the forces of life, which he describes in lively detail (1369-76). Faust, as we have seen, has two souls, which are both in him, yet also distributed between him and Mephistopheles. In an odd way even Mephistopheles participates in this complete doubleness of all beings in nature, in that he is "the spirit who always denies" (1338), for as a spirit he is part of the higher realm.

The name "devil" is warranted not by Mephistopheles' separation from the cosmos but by his attitude toward it. As the naysayer, he is the part of nature that is chaotic because it is not ordered by the divinity that it denies. In terms of the neoplatonist dialectic of spirit and world, he represents the principle of world—physical reality not ordered by any spark of spirit. In the *Prologue in Heaven* the Lord said he was part of a larger plan for keeping man active. His function in the play will be to make the world accessible to Faust.

Nevertheless, it is easy for Mephistopheles to steal the show, especially since the Lord is so tolerant. For obvious reasons a devil in rebellion against an oppressive divine order appealed to romantics writing in the wake of the French Revolution. Eighteenth-century rationalism robbed the devil of his metaphysical force,[4] and Goethe was among the first to interpret Satan in *Paradise Lost* (1667) as a kind of revolutionary hero. Even though Milton's devil is less entertaining than Goethe's, many readers since 1800 have also wanted to see him as the real hero of the epic. Is Mephistopheles the hero of *Faust*, the natural rising against an outmoded and rigid order? The greatest difficulty with such an interpretation lies, it seems to me, in the instability of the point of view in the play. Such an exclusive focus on Mephistopheles makes Faust fade into insignificance, and fixes our sympathies and understanding in ways that we have seen are impossible in *Faust*. By rejecting order Mephistopheles offers a freedom from constraint that is essential to every human being. In that respect a revolutionary reading of Mephistopheles is entirely justified. But every human being has two souls, so that in addition to the freedom of the world, the higher order of the mind is also necessary. Here the revolutionary reading breaks down and needs to become dialectical.

REPRESENTATION AS MEDIATION

The basic structure of *Faust* opposes longing for transcendence and longing for the world (or escape from the self and immersion in the self), both within Faust and between Faust and Mephistopheles. The neoplatonist dialectic allows the soul to perceive divine truth represented in the order of nature, and such moments do occur in the play. Faust arrives at this kind of resolution, for example, in his speech to the setting sun (1070–99): instead of moving directly outward and upward, as he wished to do earlier, he wants only to circle around the earth between the world and the heavens. Circling is the motion of the planetary spheres at the beginning of the archangels' hymn (243–45) and thus the motion of nature ordered by divine spirit. When Faust sees the world from the perspective of the sun, the divine order in it becomes visible. This resolution can be traced through Faust's other moments of insight in the first two scenes. The macrocosm was the sign of nature's orderliness; the earth spirit articulated his place in the hierarchy of nature as the weaver of the clothing of the eternal Godhead. Nature is thus the first stage of resolution of the dialectic in the play, the first place for Faust to seek that knowledge which is inaccessible to the human mind without mediation.

Nature is not, however, very concrete in Faust's brief moments of apparent communion. In the speech to the moon, Faust expresses a wish—"If only, full Moonlight, you looked" (386), "If only I could walk on the mountain heights" (392). Faust sees nothing but some murky moonbeams; nature is only in his vision, as he soon realizes. The macrocosm and earth spirit are but signs in a book Faust is looking at, not natural or real. What appears to Faust as he speaks the charm of the earth spirit is a "shape of flame" (499), an image. Similarly, the climaxes of both the resolution to commit suicide and the speech to the sunset are visions created by Faust. Especially in this last speech, he would not be immersed in nature but hovering over it, enjoying the eternal vision of it. The resolution of the tension comes consistently in a representation of nature in vision or sign; the nature in which transcendent order is visible is constructed by the human imagination.

How can projections of Faust's own imagination enable him to escape his own subjectivity for the otherness of the object? or enable him to escape the toils of the world for higher truth? Faust himself sees this problem only too clearly, as his visions fade or are recognized to be only "play" (454). But in this text ecstatic visions always respond to some outward stimulus—the moonlight, signs in a book, the vial of poison, the setting sun. And with each of these objects it is light that first catches Faust's attention. We have already seen that the reflection on the vial of poison makes Faust think first of moonlight, the sign of the macrocosm seems to make everything bright (439), and the earth spirit appears in a flame. (Compare the beginning of the archangels' hymn, where the light of the sun evokes the ineffability of the Godhead.) As in the Hebrew prophets of the Old Testament, light is the objective manifestation of spiritual presence too bright for human eyes. Faust's visions really do connect something outside to his inner self.

In *Night* Faust is not yet able to appreciate this mediation. He is disappointed to find himself in his study when he thought he was dancing with spirits in the moonlight, and turns from the macrocosm because it is "only a play" (454). When Wagner mistakes Faust's encounter with the earth spirit for a play being declaimed, Faust inveighs ferociously against drama. Wagner was, of course, correct, for the earth spirit is an image in the flame. He cannot be real in the sense that Faust is real, since spirit is by definition not physically real. Faust reveals a limitation in himself, not a limitation in play. If he had been able to see his encounter with the earth spirit as a play of great significance, he would not have been rejected by it, because he would have comprehended it. At this point Faust takes representations to be realities, and not illusions that can nevertheless communicate higher truth.

He makes some progress in the later parts of the sequence under discussion. The chorus of angels (starting at line 737) that deflects him from suicide is composed of human singers, and he accepts it without disappointment. What he overhears is the Easter sequence, the earliest of the medieval church plays that begin the continuous dramatic tradition of Western Europe. Similarly, he knows his last speech to the sunset is only a wish, but it does not upset him as wishing did at the beginning of *Night. Faust* will be the record of its hero's progress as a reader: the final speech of Part II begins, "Everything transient / Is only a likeness" (12104–5). Nature and art will become indistinguishable as mediators between self and other, and all reality will represent higher truth.

Only when Faust has achieved enough understanding of representation to accept his distance from the sun at the end of *Before the City Gate* does Mephistopheles set foot on stage. What has he—what has Goethe—been waiting for? The text never explains, so we must ask instead: What does it say about Mephistopheles that he does not appear in the play until Faust has learned to accept representations? This question is its own answer: Mephistopheles can have no impact on Faust unless Faust accepts representations, for representations are all Mephistopheles has to offer!

Mephistopheles is above all a purveyor of illusions. The devil is traditionally known as the "prince of lies," and Faust expects no more when he first meets him. Even the Lord described him as a "rogue" (339) in the *Prologue*. In his first exchange with Faust Mephistopheles calls attention to his slipperiness with words: no sooner has Faust asked his name than Mephistopheles questions the validity of a word to characterize an essence. He mocks, of course, Faust's angry denunciation of words at the beginning of *Night*, and his more recent rejection of "word" to translate *logos*, but in so doing he places the problem of how words represent at the center of the discussion. Consider also the one proof he gives Faust of his power before they make their pact: his spirits sing to Faust. The song describes no special luxuries or demonic temptations, but a beautiful landscape instead. Since Faust has just engaged in the same kind of nature description at his moments of closest approach to higher truth, Mephistopheles projects the same kinds of illusions as Faust. Over and over in the play Mephistopheles will stage little plays (in *Auerbach's Cellar* and *Witch's Kitchen*) and provide props to further the action when Faust is the lead actor (in the seduction of Margarete and the later abduction of Helena). As the principle of the material world, and as the aspect of Faust that clings to the real world, Mephistopheles provides the materials on which Faust's restless imagination will operate.

Let us be clear on the powers at the disposal of this devil-impresario. In the Faust legend Faust summons Mephistopheles by magical powers and receives from him more elaborate magical powers. Goethe's Faust turns to magic in his opening monologue but does not even use it to conjure Mephistopheles. When he and Mephistopheles set off on a magic carpet (actually Mephistopheles' cloak) at the end of the second *Study* scene, the devil explains that it travels on heated air (2069–70). Since the hot air balloon had just been invented in 1783, this is the latest in scientific explanations. Mephistopheles is, after all, the principle of physical reality: whether scientific or not, all of Mephistopheles' magic involves illusionary manipulation of the natural world. His magic is natural, not supernatural.

But the creation of illusions is precisely the function of theater. Magic is a metaphor for the dramatic activity of the poet himself. As the magic carpet gets Faust out of his study faster than walking would, magic is a convenient shortcut for processes that would otherwise take too long. Mephistopheles will say as much to Faust when he persuades him to drink an elixir of youth in *Witch's Kitchen*: Faust can drink the potion or dig in a field for 80 years to stay healthy and fit (2352–61). Similarly, Margarete falls in love with Faust faster because of the jewels provided by Mephistopheles' magic, but there can be no doubt that the affair would have taken the same course, though not at the same pace, without the devil's services. The shortcut is less for Faust than for Goethe: magic is a convenient mechanism to compress many different events into a play that constitutes three long evenings in the theater. The dramatic poet purveys illusions, just as the devil does, a similarity long since recognized by sixteenth- and seventeenth-century religious polemicists against the theater. There is even a perspective, then, in which Mephistopheles must be identified with Goethe himself; he is an image of the poet in his own play.

This interpretation of magic in the play brings the argument full circle to Faust again. For Faust's longing to transcend the world and perceive higher truth is inexorably deflected into moments of representation of nature, and now it turns out that this is precisely the skill that Mephistopheles can bring to Faust. In Part II Mephistopheles will openly serve as master of ceremonies, director, and even dramatic coach to an increasingly willing and adept Faust. It is small wonder, then, that the two have no difficulty reaching agreement, and that their pact can ultimately lead to the salvation predicted in the *Prologue in Heaven*.

THE WAGER

The beginning of the second *Study* scene reiterates the importance of the world to Faust's striving and adjusts the terminology once more. Mephistopheles arrives at a moment of despair for Faust. Despair is the negative version of his striving, for he wishes that he had died in the moment that the earth spirit appeared to him (1577–78). His problem is less the emptiness of life than the impermanence of those fulfilling moments of ecstasy. In this mood he curses all the things in life that might cause a person to strive; this is truly his lowest moment. But no moment is ever stable in *Faust*. A chorus of invisible spirits mourns the destructiveness of Faust's curse and encourages him to rebuild the world. Mephistopheles claims these spirits as his own and adds further encouragement to stop moping and be a man. He does just what God had said he would do for Faust: keep him from being lazy. Mephistopheles may be working in his own interest here, but he is also functioning as part of a larger dialectical plan. And sure enough, Faust bounces right back. No sooner does Mephistopheles offer his services in this life in exchange for Faust's in the next, than Faust professes utter indifference to anything beyond this life. This return to the world repeats the effect of the Easter chorus from *Night* in a different key, for Faust embraces life again and also re-affirms the divinity of his striving. "Has your sort," he scornfully asks Mephistopheles, "ever comprehended the human spirit in its noble striving?" (1676–77). Mephistopheles has nothing of value to offer him, he continues, because Mephistopheles can offer him nothing lasting—food, gold, women's love, honor all disappear. As in the previous depression, value is determined by permanence, and permanence is associated with man's higher striving, with what separates him from the worldly devil. Eternity is now another name for what Faust perceived as divine in *Night.*

In his eagerness to silence Mephistopheles on this point, Faust transforms the devil's offer of a pact into a wager: if Mephistopheles ever offers anything that seems worthy to Faust of being permanent, Mephistopheles may carry off Faust's soul. The essence of this wager is time. Its key term is that Faust should never say to the passing moment, "Tarry a while, thou art so fair" (1700); and, Faust continues, if he ever does so, "The clock may stand fast, the pointer fall, / Let time be over then for me!" (1705–6). And when the wager is concluded Faust exclaims, "Let us plunge into the rushing of time, / Into the rolling of happenstance!" (1754–55). Time has always been of the essence in the Faust legend, in which Faust was originally offered a term of 24 years before he would have to surrender himself, body and soul, to the devil. Goethe has, however, made an important change here, for Faust is to have all the time in the world, or at least all the time he does not like. Time will last for him as long as he chooses to live and seek new forms of action (remember that "deed" was his final translation for *logos*). The issue is really whether he will ever stop striving.

Memory was already important in the prologues and to some extent in *Night*, where the concern was to recover the past—that is, to give it a certain permanence. Permanence was a problem, we remember, for historicism, which had called the permanent significance of the past into question for the first time in European thought. In a dialectical response to historicism's denial of the past, Goethe transforms the past into an inaccessible ideal, something categorically desirable but not attainable in the transience of the world. Whereas earlier in the play time concerned individuals in relation to their personal pasts, the theme is now extended to the place of the human mind in time.

In this generalized version of the historicist dialectic, it begins to look very much like that of world and spirit. In fact, the natural world is traditionally subject to change in time, while God exists permanently above and outside of it. To locate man between temporality and permanence is the same as locating him between nature and transcendence. And indeed, the language of the wager, "If I ever say to the moment, tarry a while," suggests as much. The German word for moment, *Augenblick*, means literally "glance of the eye." If we remember the importance of light for triggering Faust's attention in his ecstatic moments in *Night* and *Before the City Gate*, the implied pun connects *moment* with Faust's earlier moments of transcendence. Thus the terms of the wager readily translate from fulfilled moment to perception of higher truth in the world.

Nevertheless, the shift to temporal terms introduces a new element. Faust has already had momentary experiences of transcendence (this is why he wishes he had died in the moment of seeing the earth spirit). The bet is not that there will never be such moments but that Faust will never wish for them to last. Why should Faust not want such moments to last? In the superficial context of the discussion between Faust and Mephistopheles the answer is obvious. So long as Mephistopheles offers empty, transient pleasures of the world, of course Faust is too noble, his goals are too high, for the devil to understand and have anything of lasting value to offer. But having interpreted the wager in terms of the dialectic of world and spirit, we can see on the basis of the earlier scenes that Mephistopheles has much of value to offer; for only in the world can inaccessible higher truth be represented, and Mephistopheles, in giving Faust access to the world and to a world of representations, will mediate between him and the transcendence he seeks.

So again we must ask why the moment should not last. Now the issue is not Faust's innate nobility but the connection of the neoplatonist to the historicist dialectic. In the wake of historicism it is impossible to exist both in and out of time, to be both in and out of the world simultaneously. In effect Mephistopheles has offered Faust access to transcendence, and Faust knows intuitively that at best Mephistopheles can offer only temporary representations of it, because that is all that can be offered in the world. No illusion can be permanent, for it ceases to represent something other than itself when it becomes a seamless part of the real world.

Hence it is obvious that Mephistopheles cannot win the bet, just as it was clear in the *Prologue in Heaven* that he had no chance of winning his bet against God. The psychology of the situation may seem improbable to some readers, who wonder how anyone could believe that Mephistopheles would be so stupid. But Mephistopheles is not stupid; the problem lies rather in our expectations that there is any psychology to the situation. Mephistopheles, charming and urbane as he often is, is not the mimetic representation (or imitation) of a real person; he is an allegorical representation of the principle of worldliness and denial of spirit. Sometimes he seems to understand his place in the larger hierarchy of the natural order, as, for example, when he calls himself "part of the power, / That always wills evil and always achieves good" (1335–36). But such insight cannot affect his behavior, for then he would cease to be what he is. As if to emphasize this point Goethe has Mephistopheles insist that their agreement be signed in blood, while Faust laughs, for he has joined Mephistopheles precisely to get away from narrow-minded "word-mongering." Now Mephistopheles is the pedant, like Wagner, while Faust is the figure with some divine spark.

The terms of the wager are also important from the point of view of the subject-object dialectic. Once again the crucial passage is Faust's saying to the moment, "Tarry a while, thou art so fair." Goethe did not invent this phrase; he borrowed it from the fifth promenade in Rousseau's *Reveries of a Solitary Wanderer*, published in 1782 and immediately a famous and influential text. Sounding remarkably like Faust, Rousseau says, in the middle of a tirade about the emptiness and transience of human existence, "In our most vivid joys there is scarcely an instant at which our hearts could truly say: *Would that this moment might last forever.*"[5] He goes on to imagine what such a moment would consist of, and decides it would mean lying in a boat floating gently on a lake with neither external stimuli nor any succession of internal sentiments to mark the passage of time. The highest moment for Rousseau is the moment of pure consciousness of self, that is, of pure subjectivity. When Faust insists that there can be no such moment for him, he is rejecting the subjectivity cultivated by Rousseau. For pure subjectivity in the terms of *Faust* is isolation from the world and from God; it is pure solipsism. In the personal creation myth Goethe offers in his autobiography, *Poetry and Truth,* Lucifer falls by forgetting that God is outside of himself, and his damnation is to be in a state of total self-absorption.[6] Since the beginning of the play subjectivity has been a prison to be escaped, not a state to be cultivated. Consider also Rousseau's image: one achieves the highest moment by lying still and floating. This is exactly the opposite of *Faust*, where striving is so important that it constitutes one's humanity and can earn divine forgiveness. In this sense the bet with Mephistopheles will provide Faust with unlimited access to objects and offer him escape from the prison of the self.

In all respects then, Faust should enter into whatever temptations Mephistopheles offers him. He does not have to wallow in them—indeed, he must not—but to reject one at any point would be to say that the previous moment should last. To the extent that Faust should enter into the wager with Mephistopheles at all (and the *Prologue* has provided a context in which he should), the bet shows clearly and explicitly that human striving must be dialectical, that it must embrace the opposite of what it seeks in order to achieve its goals. To achieve permanence Faust must plunge into temporality, to find transcendence he must look into the world, to be at one with himself he must embrace what is not himself.

But how can it be right for Faust to make a pact with the devil? No matter how clearly Goethe has redefined the terms of the situation, no matter how amusing his undermining of traditional religious patterns, the question still presses, for the religious patterns are too powerful simply to be laid aside. Goethe has made his play much harder to understand by redefining so deeply rooted an image in our culture. The devil is the embodiment of evil, and no matter how often we remind ourselves that evil is part of the natural order for Goethe, we either slip and misread the play or else feel very uncomfortable with the idea that Faust must fall into every temptation and not be delivered from evil, contrary to the Lord's Prayer, in order to be saved.

And it is right to feel uncomfortable. The scene between Mephistopheles and the student draws a parallel between the pact scene and the fall of Adam and Eve in Genesis. After a satirical attack on the state of learning in German universities (1868–2000), as applicable in Goethe's day as in Faust's, Mephistopheles steers the student toward medicine because it offers such lovely opportunities to enjoy life (in the form of female patients). Here is another parallel between the student and Faust, because Mephistopheles will shortly become his go-between to Margarete. Furthermore, Mephistopheles turns the student away from book learning and toward experience in the world, just as he will lead Faust out into the real world of time. But notice what he writes in the student's autograph book: "Eritis sicut Deus scientes bonum et malum" (2048; "You shall be like gods, knowing good and evil"). These are the words of the serpent to Eve as he tempts her to eat the apple (Genesis 3:5). Even as he parodies Faust's lust for knowledge with the student's more earthly lust, Goethe has carefully underlined the problematic moral implications of Faust's pact and the perspective on temptation that it implies.

Once again the play confronts us with opposing perspectives on its central issue. It would be much easier not to have these two perspectives, to have only the traditional Faust legend, or to have only Goethe's modern redefinition of it. But both perspectives are there, and the two are in conflict with one another. We have seen repeatedly that *Faust* is a play about the difficulty of knowing, about the ineffability of truth. These same difficulties apply to moral knowledge as to other kinds of knowledge. It is probably the most important and most direct embodiment of the central problem in *Faust* that it constantly confronts us with moral contradictions.

7

The World Theater of Part I

The rest of Part I shows us Faust's adventures in the world—the seduction of Margarete and the Walpurgis Night. Goethe did not, to be sure, invent the tragedy of the seduced maiden or the witches' sabbath, but he was the first to forge the powerful combination of these elements with the Faust theme, inspiring opera upon opera and permanently changing the shape of the Faust legend. This chapter and the two that follow are intended to show how the patterns identified in the previous chapters relate these innovative sections of the play to one another and to what has come before. This section, too, is organized into a series of opposed pairs, usually with Faust and Mephistopheles, sometimes with Margarete and Mephistopheles, and sometimes with Margarete and Faust representing the opposing poles. In order to emphasize this pattern it seems most helpful first to consider the theatricality of the action, then to explore the three different types of plays contained in Part I—plays of the world, of nature, and of society.

THEATRICALITY

Mephistopheles' magic is largely theatrical, so that much of Part I consists of conjuring performances. In this regard Goethe draws on a venerable tradition going back to the Renaissance of magicians staging theater: Prospero in Shakespeare's *Tempest* is the most famous example, but several early scientists were reputed to be magicians and earned fame creating magical stage illusions.[7] Today magicians practice exclusively as showmen in Western culture. So ingrained is our expectation that magicians perform that we may overlook this aspect too quickly in *Faust*.

In Part I Mephistopheles is the entertainer complete with satin cape. In *Auerbach's Cellar*, for example, he performs a typical mountebank's trick when he makes wine flow from the table. He never intends to tempt Faust with tavern life—no one would expect wine to satisfy Faust's longing—but to demonstrate his art. Mephistopheles explicitly tells Faust he is to learn from seeing (2160), and even remarks that since the wine will be terrible, they can have come only for entertainment (2186–87). In *Witch's Kitchen* Mephistopheles stages another little play, this time a morality in which the apes crown him king of the world. Even when he is not actually in a play Mephistopheles plays a role: the witch does not recognize him when she arrives because he is dressed as a modern baron, not in the familiar costume with horns and tail. To be sure, in this historicist world even the devil's appearance changes with time, but Mephistopheles consciously adjusts to changes in fashion and chooses how he will look. He always plays a role. Even in the Gretchen Tragedy, as the scenes about Margarete are known (Gretchen is the diminutive form of Margarete), Mephistopheles suggests that the jewels he fetches for Faust's beloved are so much magical entertainment. An infatuated fool like that, he says, "Will blow you up sun, moon, and stars / To entertain his girl." (2862–64). Mephistopheles does not exactly stage the great show of the *Walpurgis Night* himself, but it is clearly a show (Faust participates in no rituals, for example) performed by Mephistopheles' fellow agents of denial, and Mephistopheles is clearly Faust's guide.

More important, Mephistopheles seems to act as director. In *Witch's Kitchen* he prepares a role for Faust. Until now Faust has been the elderly scholar, but here Mephistopheles gives him an elixir of youth to prepare him for his role as the passionate lover of Margarete. In the Gretchen Tragedy itself he directs Faust's actions: he prescribes the lie about neighbor Martha's husband, he provides the sleeping potion for Margarete's mother, he prompts Faust stroke by stroke in the fatal duel with Margarete's brother Valentine. Where Mephistopheles does not perform, he directs the plays-within-the-play.

Where Mephistopheles is the performer, Faust is his audience. In the original manuscript Faust performed the tricks in *Auerbach's Cellar*, but as we have it now, Faust's role is exclusively to watch. Similarly, in *Witch's Kitchen* Faust has nothing to do but watch the apes dress Mephistopheles up and then watch the witch perform her ridiculous hocus-pocus. He does, to be sure, drink the potion at the end of the scene, but as discussed in chapter 10 of this book, drinking is consistently associated with seeing and knowing; thus it too is a kind of watching. None of this action seems any more serious to Faust than the antics of the previous scene, but otherwise he looks at the image of a beautiful woman in a magic mirror, another magic show put on for his entertainment. In the *Walpurgis Night's Dream* at the end of the *Walpurgis Night* Faust and Mephistopheles end up at a play in honor of the golden wedding anniversary of Titania and Oberon, the fairy king and queen from Shakespeare's *Midsummer Night's Dream*. Not only have they somehow stumbled into a different play, but they also end up watching one. This fact is especially remarkable because Faust expected to meet Satan himself, who is supposed to be holding court at the top of the mountain. Goethe was up to creating Satan's court; there are even extant drafts for the scene. Nevertheless, he chose to have Faust watch an odd little play full of satirical details about Goethe's own contemporaries instead. Evidently, watching theatricals is central to the meaning of Part I.

These plays continue the trajectory of the earlier scenes, in which Faust kept looking at glimmering lights and representations of nature. Now these are elaborated into dramas such as the human mind, not just God, can construct. In giving Faust access to the world, as he promises in the pact, Mephistopheles offers Faust materials with which to represent higher truth to himself so that he can perceive it. Faust must first learn to read, then to create representations that embody not Mephistopheles' view but the order of higher truth toward which Faust himself strives.

PLAYS OF THE WORLD

The first two plays Faust watches may be loosely characterized as plays of the world, with *world* understood in the strictly physical sense. In both *Auerbach's Cellar* (cellars of public buildings are still traditional locations for taverns in Germany) and *Witch's Kitchen*, Faust is shown a thoroughly disorderly subhuman world without a spark of divine order. *Witch's Kitchen* is peopled by apes, *Auerbach's Cellar* by drunkards who happily listen to songs about rats and fleas, and who themselves sing, "We feel so cannibalistically good, / Just like five hundred sows!" (2293–94). This is the world Mephistopheles knows and loves, the place where "bestiality [is] magnificently revealed" (2297–98). When he distributes literal alcoholic *spirits* to drink (the same pun operates in German as in English), the drinkers rise to a moment of higher vision in which ordinary, ugly things like noses seem to be beautiful grapes; this is Mephistopheles' parody of the harmonization of spirit and world for which Faust yearns. The two leave, avoiding the inevitable disillusionment that follows. As in *Night*, Faust has not attempted to interpret the play.

Witch's Kitchen starts with the same world, but its version of the dialectic goes further because Faust himself is the drinker. The world has more shape here in that Mephistopheles and the apes perform a little play: the apes crown him king, and indeed the devil is king of the strictly temporal world devoid of divine order. The motifs of chance (2394–99) and the fragility and emptiness of the world (2402–15) emphasize the chaos here. The witch's brew, offered with pseudomathematical incantation, parodies divine order, as do the alcoholic spirits in the previous scene.

But Faust provides a more serious element of divine order as he gazes at the beautiful figure in the magic mirror. The image may well be the creation of the devil, but even so it inspires Faust to the same yearning for truth that characterized his highest moments in *Night*. It is a "divine image" (2429), the "paradigm of all heavens" (2439). Regardless of its origins, Faust makes it represent the ideal. Now he embodies, as so often in *Night*, the soul that strives upward, and Mephistopheles the one that clings to the world. The witch interrupts his ecstasy, but her potion will lead him to a higher state still. Drinking suggests that Faust internalizes and perceives in some totalizing fashion what has passed. More important, he has also shaped the action with his rhetoric of the ideal, so that he participates much more than in *Auerbach's Cellar*. The results of the potion appear in the Gretchen Tragedy, where Faust not only joins but also often directs the action.

The problem of subjectivity also structures these scenes. The morose Faust of *Auerbach's Cellar* does not engage with the world but remains enclosed in his own subjectivity. In *Witch's Kitchen*, too, he remains aloof from Mephistopheles, the witch, and the apes center-stage; only late in the scene is he drawn into communication with the rest of the world as he drinks the potion. But then Faust accosts Margarete on the street, for the time being, at least, no longer imprisoned in his subjectivity. Thus, these two scenes recapitulate the development of the action up through the pact. In fact, since both were written by 1788, the first part of *Faust* really elaborates what was implicit in these two little plays of the world.

Consider how this context affects the moral implications of the scenes. One's first instinct is to cheer Faust for ignoring the devil's temptations. But Mephistopheles makes no effort to engage Faust's interest in *Auerbach's Cellar*; he only wants, as he says at line 2297, to show him the bestiality of the world. The drinkers, of course, are punished for accepting the temptations of the devil—or are they? Mephistopheles has warned them not to spill any wine, and no one is burned until it is spilled. The message is not to avoid the gifts of the devil, but to use them carefully. In the same way *Witch's Kitchen* is a chaotic, tiresome place, but it is disappointingly undemonic and undangerous. Such is Faust's situation as defined by the pact: he may use the gifts of the world safely, as long as he does so in the service of a higher ideal, as long as he strives.

PLAYS OF NATURE

If Part I contains a natural and a supernatural play about the world, it also contains plays about natural and supernatural nature: *Forest and Cavern* and the *Walpurgis Night*. Like our first two, one is dominated by Faust, the other by Mephistopheles. Because both scenes interrupt the Gretchen Tragedy, they function as temporary escapes from the intensity of Faust's affair with Margarete. This is only appropriate, for nature is both the antidote and the necessary detour to Faust's yearning, which is focused for the moment on Margarete. With these opposing perspectives we are within the familiar pattern.

At first *Forest and Cavern* seems to show Faust's longing for nature fully satisfied. The sublime spirit addressed at the beginning of the scene is usually taken to be the earth spirit from *Night*. If so, the passage suggests Goethe may once have intended a larger role for the earth spirit as the opposite perspective on nature from Mephistopheles, who dominates this scene after Faust's mood shifts from positive to negative. At this point it hardly matters who the spirit is or what the spirit did, for the view of nature is actually controlled by Faust's rhetoric and will change with his mood. For the moment, at least, he has temporarily created an image of nature that reflects higher order.

Faust is at peace here, as he was intermittently in *Night*, and feels at one with nature. This is a moment of resolution that allows him total vision (3224) and also frees him from subjective isolation, for nature is his brother (3226) and friend (3224). When storms come and he withdraws into his cave, the moment is heightened: there the spirit shows him to himself, and the secrets of his own breast are revealed (3232–34). Withdrawal into the cave is the equivalent of withdrawal into himself, so that there is no longer any difference between nature and the self. The cave also permits recovery of the past into the present, for there "The silver forms of early days appear, / And soften the stern pleasure of reflection." (3238–39). All three dialectics—of nature, of the self, of time—are temporarily resolved through Faust's own imagination, which projects the cave, the memories, and the peace.

Before Faust's mood changes, as it will in the next line, it is worth comparing this experience to his various moments of apparent communion with nature in *Night*. This experience differs in its more substantial sense of possession, in its calm, and in its apparent stability. But is it any more valid? That Faust claims to have received this communion from the earth spirit who rejected him in *Night* might seem to undermine the experience. But given the care with which Goethe prepared this text for publication, it would not be legitimate to assume that he forgot to write an additional scene in which the earth spirit relented, or that he had originally meant to take account of the earth spirit in the pact scene but forgot. Rather, these lines suggest that Faust is in communion with nature now and that the language available to him to articulate it is "the gift of the great spirit." He is in fact out of doors in a landscape that looks like the one he first longed for as he addressed the moon at the beginning of *Night*. His position in *Forest and Cavern* is the literal fulfillment of his earlier wishes in that nature is now concretely there all around him: there is something objective present to his viewing subject. In this sense it was not quite fair to ask if his vision is any more valid than earlier, for his visions in *Night* were valid in that they were always evoked by some bright light outside of Faust. The real difference here is Faust's greatly increased control over his vision.

But his mood shifts and the moment passes, even before the devil arrives (after line 3250). Mephistopheles almost seems to come with Faust's change in mood rather than to cause it, and Faust argues as much against the feelings inside him as against this external tempter. Such reversal of mood from within Faust is typical of *Night*, but there is again an important difference, because his negative perspective is now objectified in the attendant devil. Mephistopheles wants Faust to return to the world and complete the seduction of Margarete, who, he says, longs for her lover, while Faust wants to preserve her purity. The paradox that Faust will destroy Margarete's purity by taking possession of it represents the conflict between Faust's striving for perfect truth and the need for it to be expressed in the imperfect natural world.

It would be an error to read Mephistopheles' snarly tone as a sure sign of evil that Faust should avoid, because the next scene shows that Mephistopheles is not lying about Margarete's longing for Faust. His tone contrasts with Faust's rhetoric in the first half, but Faust's nobility is tormenting his beloved. Just by attracting Margarete's attention, Faust has already involved her irremediably in her doom—"Man always errs whenever he strives," the Lord has said in the *Prologue in Heaven* (317). For the first time Faust confronts the moral complexity of his striving. This play about nature has become a play about human nature.

The *Walpurgis Night* seems rather a play about demonic nature. Faust and Mephistopheles climb a mountain to attend a witches' sabbath, and all around them witches, warlocks, and various gruesome ghosts also make their way to the summit, where Satan himself will receive them. The scene is a favorite with opera composers and with stage directors, especially because Goethe deprived them of a climactic scene in Hell (though many opera composers added one). Although the witches' sabbath is surprisingly replaced by the anniversary masque *Walpurgis Night's Dream*, the mood still does not reverse abruptly as in *Forest and Cavern*. The *Walpurgis Night* does seem to be a thoroughly Mephistophelean realm.

But nothing is ever quite what it seems in *Faust*, and this scene is no exception. Consider first its place in the drama, right after Margarete faints in the cathedral. Margarete has been persecuted there by an evil spirit and calls for fresh air: the scene is immediately transformed. Margarete vanishes, but the *Walpurgis Night* does indeed come to the audience as a breath of fresh air, with a beautiful evening landscape in place of the oppressive cathedral, and Faust's praise of nature in place of the savage hymn "Dies Irae" ("Day of Wrath"). How odd that Faust should expatiate on the beauties of the coming spring on his way to a witches' sabbath! He and Mephistopheles are led by a will-o'-the-wisp; in Goethe's "Fairy Tale" (1795) these creatures do not lead people astray but are courteous and helpful. As the three of them now sing in alternation, the description of nature becomes slightly more grotesque but never threatening. This nature is not very demonic after all.

It is also interesting to consider what all the witches and warlocks are up to in this scene. They want to reach Satan, their god, at the summit of the mountain (the main topic of their choruses in lines 3956–4015). Usually one seeks the devil below: the reversed direction calls attention to parody lurking here. For all these witches and warlocks, along with Faust and Mephistopheles, are *striving* to reach their ideal of perfection. But their ideal is the devil, not God—lies, not truth. What is the sense of the parody? That Faust's striving has now truly been perverted? Perhaps, but then why does Mephistopheles hold him back from the top of the mountain and drag him off to the banal satire of mountebanks and the *Walpurgis Night's Dream?* Mephistopheles' demonic nature is inhabited not by Satan but by the same insignificant beasts as *Auerbach's Cellar* and *Witch's Kitchen*. Mephistopheles leads Faust through a sort of market fair that is a comic Halloween version of an ordinary fair. The monsters are pretty tame after all, and the horrors are only petty obscenities. Demonic nature is banal because, as we already know, it is not ordered by higher truth, which is now represented by Satan at the summit. Even Satan can be made to represent God—that is the sense of the parody. Small wonder that Goethe aroused such anger in religious circles.

In this implicit ordering of nature, and in the apparent beauty of nature, even when it hosts a witches' sabbath, there is a double perspective comparable to the more explicit one in *Forest and Cavern*. There nature was orderly or chaotic, depending on whether Faust or Mephistopheles dominated the mood. Here nature seems to be orderly and chaotic simultaneously. This increased complexity reflects Faust's increasing participation in the representations of the world; as Faust and Mephistopheles sing together in a trio with the will-o'-the-wisp, and as Faust participates in the dances on the Brocken yet also remembers Margarete, the double perspective of nature as both chaos and representation of higher order becomes increasingly obvious to him and to us.

The full lesson of this pattern is drawn by the final play-within-the-play, the *Walpurgis Night's Dream*. Goethe first wrote this play as a satirical attack (whose objects are identified in most commentaries on the play) and only decided to include it in *Faust* when his friend and collaborator Schiller hesitated to publish it alone. It is nevertheless highly relevant to *Faust* because of its ironic theatricality; it keeps breaking its own illusion. For the masque is actually a play-within-the-play-within-the-play, and it is repeatedly interrupted by figures from its frames, from its on-stage audience, and from its own orchestra of insects. That such an incompetent production, written and performed by amateurs, can represent at all is assured by the parallel to Shakespeare's *Midsummer Night's Dream*, the last act of which involves a play about Pyramus and Thisbe staged by amateurs who, despite their incompetence, successfully entertain the nobles and summarize the central concerns of the frame play. The allusion to Shakespeare is strengthened by the otherwise inexplicable appearance, at the end, of Puck, the mischief maker of *A Midsummer Night's Dream*, and Ariel, exquisite and faithful servant to Prospero in *The Tempest* —Shakespeare's two most famous and most theatrical nature spirits. Even this totally incompetent and vapid play, like Satan, can be taken to represent higher truth.

Demonic nature or human nature, supernatural nature or natural nature—all turn out to be the same thing from different points of view. Within this constancy, however, two trends emerge. First, Faust participates more and more in shaping Mephistopheles' nature to make it less demonic and more representative of higher order. Second, the natural world becomes more and more theatrical and artificial. The *Walpurgis Night's Dream* is the next-to-the-last scene in Part I; only the last scene of the Gretchen Tragedy (whose theatricality we will discuss shortly) follows it. In this respect the *Dream* marks the border between Parts I and II. From now on art will take precedence over nature as the place in which higher truth is represented in the world.

THE PLAY OF SOCIETY

Faust seems to start afresh with the Gretchen Tragedy: tone, pacing, form, meter, plot, language all change abruptly from what has gone before. There is good reason for this perception. Except for *Forest and Cave*, the *Walpurgis Night*, and a very few inserted lines here and there, this material was all written for the *Urfaust* in the mid-1770s. Some scenes now in verse were in prose in the original version, but the conversion involved no substantial changes in content. So different is this section of the drama that some scholars consider this the "real" *Faust* and the rest not-always-compatible addition. But such shifts are in fact typical in the play and not unusual at all. There are substantial shifts in tone, form, plot, and meter among the prologues, and again between larger groups of scenes—certainly between the prologues and *Night*, between *Study* and *Auerbach's Cellar*. Each of these breaks signals a deeper penetration into the play, a passing from a frame into a play within it, and a passage into a new perspective.

Perhaps the most striking difference between this part of the play and earlier ones is scene length. Until now the play has been composed of substantial, more or less self-contained scenes. Now suddenly comes a series of brief flashes, which are not always clearly linked causally or even sequentially. In the 1770s this style was considered Shakespearean, since many of Shakespeare's histories and tragedies contain such short scenes. Goethe was the most famous exponent of Shakespearean style in Germany at the time, and his historical drama *Götz von Berlichingen* started a fad for it in

1773. Nevertheless, Shakespeare used this technique for battles, not for love stories, so the direct historical explanation is insufficient. But the context of the play offers another kind of explanation: the fragmentariness of the Gretchen Tragedy directly represents the chaos and disorder of the world into which Mephistopheles leads Faust, and thus corresponds to the chaos of the world in *Auerbach's Cellar* and *Witch's Kitchen*.

Each time the play has changed levels there has also been a sense of characters changing identity or taking on new roles—for example, the harlequin seemed to become Mephistopheles, the speaker of *Dedication* seemed to become the poet in the *Prelude*, and Faust's rejuvenation in *Witch's Kitchen* seemed to prepare him for his new role as seducer in the Gretchen Tragedy. This is the first time, however, that a character has kept the same name in crossing from one level of the play to the next. If Faust can be seen changing from philosopher to seducer before our very eyes, that change undermines confidence in dramatic identity in the play. But actually, how stable was Faust's identity previously? In *Night* his mood changed constantly, while his yearning remained constant. God had already said in the *Prologue* that amidst his erring a good man nevertheless remains conscious of the right way (328–29). This reminds us that Mephistopheles' identity also remains constant across the barrier from the *Prologue* to *Study*, although he disappears for a while in between, changes form several times, and also seems to change function. Amidst constant changes in mood and role there remains some irreducible core of identity. In Faust's case it is his striving.

The Gretchen Tragedy has always had a compelling, direct emotional impact on its audiences. For this reason it can be hard to accept the idea that, like Mephistopheles' antics in *Auerbach's Cellar*, it is a play-within-the-play . It is not clear, in any case, that it did function as a play-within-the-play in the *Urfaust*. Goethe's great genius in revising the first version was to maintain the naive emotional appeal in the seduction of Margarete while he framed it in such a way that it also became ironically theatrical. As something that simultaneously feels real yet is obviously the projection of a poet, the Gretchen Tragedy is the most sophisticated example in *Faust* of the resolution of the dialectic of subject and object.

This point is so important that the self-consciously theatrical aspects of these scenes must be clarified before they can be interpreted. Mephistopheles' role as director and stage manager, discussed earlier, is enhanced by the abrupt shift from the preceding scenes. Although the shift derives from the different times and moods in which the parts were written, Goethe has exploited this necessity to set the Gretchen Tragedy apart as an inset piece. It also contains inserted songs, even whole scenes that are only sung or declaimed (e.g., Gretchen at her spinning wheel) or that are written in individual meters, like *Keep*, which is a prayer. As a whole the Gretchen Tragedy bears remarkable resemblance to several operettas that Goethe wrote in the 1770s and 1780s, both in its use of domestic settings and in the unexpected reversal to a happy ending in a prison setting (here a voice calls out that Margarete is saved). The casting is also typical of operetta of the period in that it contrasts a serious pair of lovers, Faust and Margarete, with a comic pair, Mephistopheles and Martha; the elaborate juxtaposition of the two love conversations as the pairs stroll around the stage in *Martha's Garden*, almost in an elaborate dance, calls attention to this aspect. It is no wonder that *Faust* has been adapted as an opera by so many composers, for they were responding to the innately operatic nature of Goethe's plot.

What, now, does Faust make this play represent? The best place to look for an answer is where he intervenes in the action. First he chooses Margarete, then he creates her character before he becomes acquainted with her. She has spoken only one line to Faust, and only told the audience how attractive she finds Faust, when he falls madly in love with her, visits her room—in her absence—and tells the audience all about her purity and about her family life. The remarkable thing is that Margarete then seems to correspond so exactly to the portrait he has drawn; she is largely his creation.

Faust's version of Margarete is most clearly revealed in the scene in which Faust visits her room, *Evening*. His first speech,

> Welcome, sweet *twilight*,
> You who permeate this sanctuary!
> Seize my heart, sweet *pain* of love,
> You who live thirsting on the *dew* of hope!
> (2687–90, emphasis mine),

closely echoes that first longing speech to the moonlight,

> Oh that you gazed, full *moonlight*,
> For the last time upon my *pain*,
> . . .
> Oh that I could . . .
> Bathe to health in your *dew*!
> (386–97, emphasis mine)

The echoes of "light" and "pain," which are arranged to rhyme in the German, are particularly conspicuous: Margarete represents the same thing to Faust as the moonlight.

Faust ends his first speech in Margarete's room with "In this prison what bliss!" (2694). His study was a prison to him in *Night* (note also the parallel scene names *Evening* and *Night*) but hardly a blissful one. Now Faust no longer feels separated from the nature represented by the moonlight and by Margarete, so that the speech promises not the repetition but the fulfillment of his earlier wishes. The lavish religious vocabulary of the whole passage, and the emphasis on order—Margarete is the spirit of order (2702–03)—confirm this reading. When she later catechizes her lover (*Martha's Garden*, 3413–70) the connection to religion is explicit; the fact that she cared for her infant sister, and thus was a virgin mother, implicitly emphasizes the same symbolism. Margarete embodies the order of spirit, and she is the ideal, the Kantian object that liberates the subject from himself. In Faust's dream about her as a small child pressing up to the leather arm chair in which he sits, she becomes as well the pure, inaccessible past that the poet of the *Prelude* longs for, and the childhood Faust himself thinks of when he hears the Easter chorus. Faust makes Margarete embody the object of his striving in terms of all the dialectics in the play. She is the ideal—purity, truth, order, the past, the objective other.

Through Margarete this whole complex of concerns receives a new name in the play—love. To call God love may hardly seem original, but it still bears reflection. Indeed, Goethe's achievement lies less in originality than in reinvesting the obvious with profundity. In this case the renaming not only suggests that love of God is the one path from the world to God but also opens up the possibility for reciprocity. Faust must no longer strive only on his own, or only pricked by the devil from beneath, in the terms of the *Prologue in Heaven*. With love the way is open to friendly interference from above—God will lead Faust to clarity, he says in the *Prologue* (309); at the end of Part II angels will drop burning roses of love on Mephistopheles to release Faust's soul. Margarete thus becomes an opposite perspective to Mephistopheles; both make Faust strive, but Margarete by pulling from above rather than pricking from below.

This is, of course, the Faustian view of love. Like anything else that can be given a name in the play, it is subject to the Mephistophelean perspective as well. If Faust reads his love for Margarete as striving for the highest purity and truth, Mephistopheles constantly reminds him that it is seduction of the most cynical sort, for Faust has no intention of marrying her. The Mephistophelean view has been evident even before the issue is defined so explicitly in *Forest and Cavern*, before Margarete is even thought of. Mephistopheles' version of love is introduced in his exchange with the student at the end of *Study* and developed in its full glory in the songs of the rat and the flea (the latter sung by Mephistopheles himself) in *Auerbach's Cellar*. The rat, it is reported, dies of poison, "Just as if she had love in her belly" (2132); a flea is the court favorite, loved like the king's own son (2214). The full irony of Mephistopheles' song becomes clear when Margarete sings *her* famous song, "The King of Thule" (2759-82), about a king's faithful love to his dead mistress, and the audience realizes that the difference between Margarete and Mephistopheles is reduced to the difference between a dead mistress and a live flea! There is of course a difference, but in her guilt Margarete remembers with chagrin that she herself could once say ugly things about unwed mothers (*At the Well*, 3577-78). Mephistopheles' view of love as sex is as valid and necessary a view of love and of Margarete as Faust's more refined perspective. This particular version of Goethe's dialectic is perhaps more accessible to modern readers than it was to Goethe's contemporaries.

Faust does not yet read his own life in the terms outlined above. Margarete clearly represents order and purity to him, but he cannot conceive that she and Mephistopheles could be working in tandem at some higher level. He is torn rather between Margarete as an ideal and Margarete as a temptation: he must not sully her purity, but he cannot give her up. Having made her into a representation of the ideal, he then takes possession of her and thereby destroys her. In the *Prologue in Heaven* the Lord said, "Man errs as long as he strives" (317); the consequences of Faust's "error" with regard to Margarete have such devastating consequences—a manslaughter, two murders, and an execution—that Faust must for the first time confront the full moral complexity of the positive value placed on striving and on deed. The Gretchen Tragedy represents his failure to resolve these incompatible oppositions—in other words, to turn this dilemma into a dialectic.

Since the seduction is shown mostly from Margarete's perspective rather than from Faust's, it is necessary to consider the significance of the action from her perspective as well. She offers us the symmetrical version of Faust's dilemma, for she too is torn between positive and negative views of love. In *At the Well* she bewails her sinful state with the reservation, "Yet—all that drove me to it / God! was so good! ah, was so dear!" (3585–86). The temptation to physical love that was so evil to Faust seems, in Margarete's subjective view, to be pure goodness. In the eighteenth century, at least, it is inconceivable for such a good, pure soul to go astray in her feeling. Neither Faust nor the audience can really entertain the possibility. Margarete's naive virtue is good, beautiful, and true. But it is fully in accord with Mephistopheles' intentions; the temptations of this devil are subtle indeed.

At the same time the voice in Margarete that condemns her love is the voice of society, embodied in *At the Well* in Lieschen, who gleefully reports what the other girls will do to poor Barbara if she attempts to marry the father of her unborn child. Similarly, the tormenting evil spirit in *Cathedral* speaks in a loose paraphrase of the hymn being sung by the choir: it is the voice of the church. Since there is nothing attractive here about either society or the church, the bias remains very much in favor of Margarete's spontaneous submission to her love for Faust and against preserving her purity. Thus Margarete's perspective on the action conflicts fundamentally with Faust's. The moral and epistemological issues are anything but simple.

The moral paradoxes proliferate in the final scene, *Dungeon*. While Faust celebrates the Walpurgis Night with Mephistopheles, Margarete bears their child, drowns it, and is condemned to death.

Goethe in fact tried (unsuccessfully) to prevent the execution of the last woman to be beheaded for infanticide in Frankfurt (in 1772), and the Gretchen Tragedy is in part an attack on this practice. There is no question that the pathos of her insanity, her decision not to flee her punishment with Faust, and the voice from above proclaiming her salvation all enlist our sympathy. How can Margarete be saved and, ultimately, Faust also?

The issues become more complicated when the sequence of Margarete's emotions is examined in detail. Her madness at the beginning of the scene is evidently due to the murder of her infant, for she knows well enough what has happened to it as soon as she recovers. The moment Faust calls to her she comes to her senses and demands he embrace her. When she realizes that he wants only to save her, not hold her, she determines to stay and take her just punishment. Only now does her guilt prevent her from leaving the dungeon, and only now does she turn to the justice of God (4605). Her first choice for salvation is a return to Faust's love; God is her second choice. And Margarete's constancy to her lover is apparently good enough for God, for a voice from above declares her saved. The fact of love is more important than the object of love, for by taking the self beyond itself, it is a form of striving.

But why does Faust reject Margarete's love? The language leads us soon enough to an answer: her love is nothing but repetition. When Faust announces his presence she begs him, "O say it again!" (4470), and later adds, "Here is the street again, / Where I first saw you, / And the happy garden, / Where Martha and I await you" (4475–78). As Faust urgently begs her to leave she cries, "Oh tarry! / For I so like to tarry where you tarry" (4479–80). The deliberately awkward triple occurrence of *tarry* in a line and a half underlines the word, which is the key word in Faust's pact: "If I say to the moment, / Tarry a while, thou art so fair" (1699–1700). Faust has taken Margarete's love as an ephemeral thing of this world. To be sure, he made it represent something higher; that is what all who strive make of the world. But it would be wrong—in terms of his bet with Mephistopheles, in terms of our whole understanding of the world and of time in the play—to try to prolong or repeat that experience. From Faust's perspective Margarete's attempt to return to the past is a failure to strive, to develop with the current of life and accept the challenge of change.

Once again Faust and Margarete represent different perspectives on the proper conduct of human life, and both seem justified. Margarete's constancy to her love, to herself, and finally to the moral code by which she was brought up are all admirable and demand our sympathy. It is surely right for her to stay in the dungeon if Faust no longer loves her. Yet Faust's constancy to himself, to the striving that is inherent in human nature, to the change inherent in nature, is equally necessary and admirable. He is in one sense change personified, while Margarete embodies constancy. The scene portrays the tragic failure to resolve the temporal version of the dialectic, and the conflicting assertions about her fate emphasize the discordance.

One of Goethe's most famous poems is called "Constancy in Change" (*"Dauer im Wechsel"*), and it was written within a few years of the final revision of this scene. It concludes that the only permanence in human life is to be achieved in art, and in some sense the same thing happens here, because the play itself is the only framework broad enough to embrace the conflicting perspectives of hero and heroine. When Margarete cannot recover the past in her real life, and when she cannot continue to embody Faust's ideal of higher truth in real life (he is no longer in love with her), she is arbitrarily and artificially removed from the world by the voice from above. Until now that voice has seemed to be God's—it comes from above, and it proclaims salvation. But where is God in this play? Is the inaccessible, incomprehensible God celebrated by the archangels likely to interfere in this direct way? Can it be the Lord of the *Prologue*, that stagy old gardener who promised not to interfere? Why is the voice simply designated "voice" if it is that of God? The most popular operetta of the century, John Gay's *The Beggar's Opera*, ends with the author of the opera interfering at the end to save his hero from the gallows. Is it the poet who speaks here? Whoever it is, the speaker has certainly broken the illusion of the play, just as the interruptions in the *Walpurgis Night's Dream* broke the illusion there. The fact that we cannot know is part of the point. Art is our access in the world to higher truth—God—so that ultimately we hear the voice of God, whether the poet or God speaks. The important thing is that Margarete can remain what she has been to Faust only as an artificial, stagy representation. Hence the arbitrary happy end to her tragedy.

8

Part II: The Inner Perspective

At first glance Part II seems very different from Part I. The play moves from the small world to the great world in all possible respects—from the dungeon to open nature, from the confinement of the German bourgeoisie to the greatness of the imperial court, from Germany to Greece. Both Faust and Mephistopheles disappear for long stretches of the action, and our sense of reality is fractured as the play ranges across Europe over 3,000 years of history and as elves, spirits, ghosts, and monsters of all sorts take over the stage. Bizarre things happen in Part I, but the guiding presence of Mephistopheles makes the bizarre expected. In Part II neither Faust nor Mephistopheles guide the action in such obvious ways. The plot follows its own inner logic, not the causal logic of character; this is truly theater of the world.

Bizarre and independent as the world becomes in Part II, the play nevertheless continues the concerns of Part I. Although most of Part II was written between 1825 and 1831, Goethe had drafted a few speeches for acts 3 and 5, high points of Part II, during the final stages of his work on Part I. The mediation between self and world still dominates the play, and here too these oppositions have many names. The first half of Part II focuses on the inner self, the second half on the external world. Act 1 shows a descent from the real, historical world into a mysterious inner self, which is constituted from the oldest levels of the European cultural tradition in act 2, then relived up to the present of the audience in act 3. In act 4

Faust reascends to the outer historical world, while act 5 explores the consequences and difficulties of mediating between the inner and outer perspectives.

THE DIALECTIC IN PART II

Faust continues to strive all through Part II; the last scene of the play shows him still following an eternally receding ideal. But if Part I showed Faust learning to deflect his striving into the world and not to seek direct transcendence, Part II explores the various ways in which the world can be first made, then read, to represent what cannot be accessed directly by the human mind. The same opposition between world and spirit recurs in Part II, but what appeared in Part I as different kinds of plays-within-the-play appears explicitly as art of all different sorts in Part II.

This development is already clear in capsule form in the first scene, *Pleasant Landscape*. The scene opens with Faust outside among the nature spirits, precisely what he had wished for in his speech to the moon at the beginning of Part I. There he felt separate from nature, and the earth spirit rejected him. Now the spirits minister to him, and he feels in complete harmony with nature. As he watches the sun rise and call forth a rainbow from the waterfall before him, higher truth becomes visible in a form that he can articulate. Faust sees the rainbow when he turns from the blinding light of the sun coming from above (a higher light that cannot be perceived directly by human eyes) to the water coursing down the mountain (physical nature). As a colored form arising from the water of the world and the light from above the world, the rainbow is the play's most compelling image for the synthesis of world and spirit, real and ideal, and Faust identifies it as such in his final lines: "*It* reflects human striving. / Consider it, and you will comprehend more clearly: / We have our life in the colorful reflection." (4725–27). The rainbow is not only an image (in the sense of representation) of the resolution of the dialectic; it is also literally an image in that it has no substance. As this reflecting and reflected image comes under the control of the human mind in Part II, it becomes art.

Pleasant Landscape recapitulates the play's dialectic at a very abstract level. The rest of act 1 begins the process over again more concretely but still at a more general level than anywhere in Part I. The great world, in the form of the imperial court, suffers from a malaise comparable to Faust's at the beginning of *Night*. No one knows how to solve the problems of the empire, which is falling apart for lack of money, nor can anyone quite understand what is going on around him at court. As in *Auerbach's Cellar* and *Witch's Kitchen*, the court is a chaotic Mephistophelean world, meaningless because it lacks the order conferred by the presence of spirit (represented here by the missing gold that would pay the emperor's debts and the salary of his army). In a sense the entire court is in Faust's situation—longing for knowledge and understanding, and in need of the same mediation that Faust sought in Part I. The rest of Part II offers a series of mediating images, all of which are questioned as to their stability and their usefulness to the striver. In this questioning Part II goes considerably beyond Part I, which only established the necessity of such images.

Rogue Mephistopheles offers the first such image when he arranges for the emperor to guarantee paper currency with treasures buried beneath the earth. Although farmers tilling their fields in northern Europe did occasionally turn up gold artifacts buried in ancient times, and Gibbon's widely popular *The Decline and Fall of the Roman Empire* (1776–88) talks about lost treasures supposedly buried as the Roman Empire was falling to the barbarians, Goethe makes this proposal sound utterly fantastic and sinister, partly to satirize various paper money schemes that governments were floating in the wake of the French Revolution. As it does consistently in Part I, Mephistopheles' mediation looks evil, but it is striking that he is the one to speak of the "natural and spiritual powers of talented men" (4896) and of "eternally governing Nature" (4986). Mephistopheles' bills are to be representations of value inaccessible but nevertheless known to be present, just like the rainbow. Indeed, the German word for bill, *Schein*, is cognate with the English *shine* and normally means "appearance." The paper money does not revitalize the empire, but it seems to fail mainly because the courtiers and the emperor use the newly printed money to continue living in luxury. Here the focus begins to shift from representation as such to how to use representations.

Another version of the resolution is a masque performed by Faust and Mephistopheles, disguised as Plutus (Greek god of wealth) and Greed, within a larger masque performed at court to celebrate Mardi Gras. They uncannily interrupt the court's meandering entertainment with a magnificent float accompanied by its own herald, an odd parody of Shakespeare's Ariel named Boy-Charioteer. Their masque is a play-within-the-play that reveals order implicit in the world, for it seems to promise that the gold of Faust/Plutus will revitalize the social order of the empire, via Mephistopheles' paper-money scheme. In addition, Mephistopheles/Greed forms obscene shapes from molten gold on the float: as in *Forest and Cavern*, he calls attention to the lowest aspect of the creative force represented by the gold—sex. Boy-Charioteer scatters magically created golden trinkets and ornaments about, which, when the audience greedily snatches at them, come alive as insects. He is, as he himself says, an allegory of poetry, whose products may be comprehended, but not grasped with the hand. Thus the trio represents human creativity in its full range of manifestations: the crassly physical, the social, and the aesthetic. Neither the audience, left with its bugs, nor the emperor, whose beard ignites in the cauldron of molten gold that Faust/Plutus offers him, "reads" these representations aright, and their value is lost. In Part I the issue for Faust was the right way to know or understand higher truth; now the issue for everyone is how to understand representations.

Henceforth the focus shifts back to Faust, but to a Faust confronting the same issues as the great world. His version of the mediating rainbow is Helena, the most beautiful woman who ever lived. This Helena is the great-world version of Margarete, the ideal embodied in human form, and she is so important that the play recreates her three separate times. First Faust descends to the mysterious Mothers and fetches the shade of Helena (act 1); then he descends to the Underworld to fetch her again, while the seduction of Leda by the swan (the act in which Helena was conceived) is reenacted three times on stage (act 2); finally a more or less flesh-and-blood Helena appears on stage in act 3, and she is brought forward through history to marry Faust. Each of these versions of mediation explores its own status and stability.

All of them are conspicuously artificial. Faust must fetch the shade of Helena from the mysterious Mothers who sit enthroned over the "images of all creatures" (6289), and to reach them he must enter into Mephistopheles' unbelievable tale of them, first striking an "attitude" with the key he has been given (stage direction after 6293), then stamping dramatically, all the time critiqued by director Mephistopheles. Faust will bring back the shades of Paris and Helena, who will appear on a stage with its special Greek set as a play-within-the-play. In a triple sequence of visions the conception of Helena in act 2 is transformed from subjective vision to aesthetic production. It moves from Faust's sleeping dream of Leda and the swan, through his waking vision of the same scene, to the stage enactment of Homunculus pouring the flame of his existence into the water around the feet of Galatea, goddess of love and beauty, as she flashes past. Homunculus is an artificial man enclosed in a crystal vial, but he has in common with Zeus, the god hidden in the swan who takes Leda, the element of fire; Galatea, similarly, is a distant stand-in for Leda as a minor sea-goddess whom Goethe has promoted to be the successor to Venus as the goddess of love. The unlikelihood that either of these figures could represent Zeus and Leda emphasizes the artificial, representational nature of this triumphant scene, all the more so because it is also a living version of Raphael's famous painting "The Triumph of Galatea." Galatea appears as the climax to a triumphant procession of the forms in which divinity has been represented, as the spirit of water (source of all life), and as the historical successor to Venus. She thus embodies the ideal in all its manifestations—aesthetic, natural, and historical.

The Helena of act 3 is the most realistic, living representation of the ideal yet, but she is nevertheless emphatically a representation. She becomes an "image" (8881) to herself when Mephistopheles tells her all the different versions of what happened to her at Troy (8881). More important, she appears in this act first as the heroine of a Greek tragedy, speaking in Greek meters and attended by a traditional Greek chorus. Her meeting and eventual marriage to Faust are represented in a succession of literary forms moving through history from antiquity to the Middle Ages to the death of Byron in 1824. Thus she appears always as an exclusively literary figure, but an increasingly concrete and historicized one. In her the past and the literary become accessible for a brief space, making her the most explicit version of what Faust has sought throughout the play.

When Faust marries her, then, the most fundamental oppositions in the play are temporarily synthesized—past and present, classical and romantic (as the original subtitle of act 3 claims), ideal and real, artificial and real. To achieve this marriage Faust and Mephistopheles (disguised as Phorcyas) must divorce her from her setting in classical Greek tragedy, teach her to speak in modern rhymes, and, finally, create a timeless Arcadian realm in which there is no distinction between past and present—a poetic realm evoked by the power of Faust's language. This process reveals more clearly than anything else in the play the dialectical nature of Goethe's enterprise. The Helena of act 1 is an unsatisfactory manifestation of the ideal because she is only a shade with no physical substance. All of act 2 is devoted to finding a body for Helena by tracing her historical context from the beginning of classical time. The historically conditioned Faust could only embrace an equally historical form. But history imposes its own limits, one of which is that figures born millennia apart cannot embrace, except in science fiction. Thus, Faust must create a fictional context to contain Helena as well. Only by striving in these two opposed directions simultaneously—in effect, by following the dictates of his two souls from Part I—can Faust temporarily achieve the goal of his striving. Helena's historical reality in this play is simultaneously aesthetic.

The marriage of ancient and modern culminates in Euphorion, the son of Faust and Helena. Phorcyas describes him as a "little Phoebus" (9620), Greek god of poetry, and the chorus makes clear that he is also a second Hermes, Greek god of trickery and inventor of Phoebus' lyre. He thus has strong credentials as poet and as prankster, and in that sense represents the synthesis of the serious and the parodistic aspects of art in *Faust*; he embodies both the poet and the harlequin from the *Prelude in the Theater*. He also embodies Faust's two souls, for he clings to the joys of earth as he chases the maidens of the chorus, and strives upward as he climbs the rocks and tries to fly. At the end of act 3 his striving puts him off balance and he seeks to go directly upward, rejecting the real world like Faust in his more extreme moments in *Night*, seeking to know higher truth without mediation. The play has long since taught that such striving is doomed to fail: he falls to his death and thereby unravels the synthesis achieved in Faust's marriage.

These representations are unstable, and even dangerous, in various degrees: the trinkets of Boy-Charioteer turn into bugs, the gold of Plutus sets fire to the court, the shade of Helena explodes in Faust's arms. Neither Galatea nor the Helena of act 3 is dangerous in quite the same literal way, although Homunculus goes up in flames at Galatea's feet, and Faust figuratively burns with love for Helena. (Indeed, in act 5 even Mephistopheles will burn with love for the angels who steal Faust's soul from him.) Nevertheless Galatea speeds past and cannot stand still, while Helena's life with Faust speeds by in remarkably condensed form, with their son being conceived, born, growing up, and dying, all apparently in one day. Partly, then, the problem is that even representations of spirit retain so much of the power of divinity that they are too hot to touch, and partly that time in the world presses as strongly on these representations as it has on Faust himself since he made his pact with Mephistopheles. Nothing can be done about the first problem, but to deal with the second Faust makes a series of descents in search of more stable forms of representation.

THE DESCENT IN SEARCH OF FORM

If in Part I Faust locates the goal of striving above himself, in the first three acts of Part II that goal is concealed beneath the surface of things. Accordingly, act 1 shows various searches for gold—by the court to validate Mephistopheles' paper money, by the audience of the masque to satisfy its lust, by the emperor (disguised as Pan in the masque) to guarantee his power. All of these involve digging underground or at least bending over to the ground, and correspond to their debasement of striving into the physical world. This gold, however, keeps changing its shape and thus eludes the eager seekers, for none of the figures at the court but the fool recognizes that gold represents some higher presence joined with reality.

The goal becomes less worldly when Faust takes over in the last third of act 1. Now he seeks the shade of Helena, a less concrete representation of the ideal than gold, and he brings to the search his loftier understanding of its significance. As the quest becomes more abstract, so does the descent. Faust might just as well climb as descend to the Mothers, Mephistopheles tells him, for they are nowhere, in no time, and no paths lead to their realm. Faust will find there an equally abstract goal, "formation, transformation" (6287), but he himself will be invisible to the Mothers, because they see "only schemata" (6290), pure forms uncontaminated by physical being. As the embodiment of pure order or form, the Mothers are the first step in stabilizing the agile and liquid gold.

Although Faust does sink at the end of the scene, the mystery surrounding these goddesses implies that they are deep, more in the figurative than in the literal sense: they are incomprehensible, as the realm of pure spirit has been all through the play. At first Mephistopheles' tale of the Mothers seems meaningless to Faust, like the rest of Mephistopheles' world, but then he decides, "In your nothingness I hope to find the universe" (6256). If Faust has decided to bring meaning to these guardians of form, and if order will be visible in the world through the play Faust is about to stage, then the descent to the Mothers has become a descent into Faust's self. The model of creativity in this scene is essentially subjective. In Part I memory, the internalization of a real past, was repeatedly identified as the inspiration of the poet. Act 2 will objectify Faust's inspiration by connecting his memory to that of the culture.

In act 2, accordingly, this descent into the self modulates into a descent into the past. First Faust sinks into his own past as the play returns to his study of Part I, and Mephistopheles encounters there both the lice he engendered in Faust's robe when he wore it, and the student he advised, now a know-all graduate. Even Wagner is there, now a professor in his own right. Then the play descends further into the past as Faust, Mephistopheles, and the newly engendered Homunculus set off for the *Classical Walpurgis Night*, an invention of Goethe's as a parodic allusion to his own *Walpurgis Night* in Part I. There Faust and Mephistopheles encounter mythological figures from the earliest beginnings to late antiquity. Finally, Faust descends into the Underworld, repository of souls from the beginning of time, to fetch Helena. Like Orpheus he will need to bring his beloved back up into the world, but the Helena he brings back has been firmly anchored in her historical context by this plunge to the bottom of history.

This astonishing romp through the origins of European culture actually takes place in triplicate. Faust meets the centaur Chiron and occupies the same place on his back that Helena once occupied, then disappears to beg her shade from Persephone in a scene not shown; like his visit to the Mothers, this quest is an abstract quest for classical form. While he is gone the play follows Mephistopheles, who encounters a series of monsters, and finally finds the Phorcyads, three hags who share one eye and one tooth among them. He is ecstatic to have found in them the paradigm of ugliness, exactly the opposite of what Faust seeks in Helena, and he borrows their form. From now until the end of act 3 Mephistopheles appears in the form of and under the name of Phorcyas. Bizarreness often points to allegory: even Mephistopheles has quested for a classical form in act 2 and thus played the role of artist.

The third quester is Homunculus, an odd little test-tube man created by Wagner, with some unspecified assistance from Mephistopheles. He is a spark of life entirely without a natural form, and because he is artificial he must be safely enclosed in glass. Nevertheless, he is a pure example of the essence of the human spirit. "So long as I exist, I must also be doing things" (6888), he says. He also participates in Faust's dream of the conception of Helena, which he interprets to Mephistopheles. He describes Leda stepping into the water as a flame that "cools off in the fluid crystal of the wave" (6910). Helena will be produced from this union of flame and water after the seduction of Leda by the swan, but Homunculus himself will also become what is described in this image. He begins as a flame enclosed in crystal, and will enter the water at the end of act 2 to spill his flame around the chariot of Galatea. As a result of this process he will enter the great chain of physical being and acquire a literal form: what happens to him is the same process that engenders Helena, the marriage of spirit and physical form. Homunculus's path to the water leads through an allegory of physical nature, where he must choose the principle of water over fire (represented by ancient philosophers) as the source of all being. Active controversy about the relative roles of fire and water in the creation of landforms still raged among geologists in Goethe's time, so that the topic is natural form as a real scientific phenomenon.

In the delightful chaos of the *Classical Walpurgis Night*, as Faust, Mephistopheles, and Homunculus wander through a bizarre landscape on their various quests, we come to see that all three are analogues for each other. Mephistopheles has become a striver, like Faust, and pursues his own ideal of ugliness in feminine form. This is the ultimate development of the problem of perspectives in Part I. Faust and Mephistopheles are indeed two souls of the same being, and, for the duration of the Helena episode, it is impossible to see the two as adversaries. Homunculus too is a striver, and like Faust, he also turns to Mephistopheles to "shorten the paths" (6890). As a result, their various versions of the quest are functionally equivalent, and myth, history, art, and science are equally valid modes of representing the ideal. If the descent into the self has become a descent into the past of the entire culture, its result has been to map the self onto the world, and the inspiration within the self can be represented by anything in the world. With this *Faust* has developed a very broad aesthetic indeed.

THE ETHICS OF COMPREHENSION

The whole world is Faust's oyster from the very beginning of Part II. The triumphant sunrise in *Pleasant Landscape* and Faust's equally triumphant, though somewhat calmer, comprehension of the rainbow as a fleeting image of truth in the world seems to mask the tragic ethical disparities from the end of Part I. Compelled by the beauty of the poetry, *Faust* critics—regardless of their views on Mephistopheles—unanimously forget that Ariel first appeared during the *Walpurgis Night* and assume that Faust's healing is good and that the scene has nothing to do with Mephistopheles, who mysteriously reappears in the following scene. Nature apparently requires Faust to put the Gretchen Tragedy behind him and seek new objects for his striving. Similarly, the play invites us to forget about Margarete and revert to the optimistic message of the *Prologue in Heaven*—that the good man will always err but still remain conscious of the right path. The spirits seem to say something similar when they end their song with "All is open to the noble, / Who understand and quickly grasp" (4664–65). Yet there is a new factor here: understanding. The earth spirit rejected Faust in *Night*, saying, "You resemble the spirit you comprehend, / Not me!" (512–13). Can Faust now both comprehend and literally grasp? He had understood Margarete as the ideal, but when he seized her and took possession of her, he destroyed her; why do the spirits now encourage him to repeat the crime? We can only recognize that they do, and that the drama has switched from Margarete's perspective back to Faust's perspective. If Faust is to continue to live, it must be from his perspective, which involves repeated errors. He will try to avoid moral error as he continues to strive; the experience with Margarete is not without effect. But humanity is remarkable, Goethe implies, because it can recover even from such radical damage as the guilt of destroying Margarete and still go on to strive anew.

In this respect, the rainbow identifies a new version of the dialectic. Comprehending and grasping are opposite aspects of the same activity: the one spiritual and abstract, the other physical. The rainbow can be comprehended, but it cannot be seized physically; the hand that tries to grasp it will close on nothing. This poses the dilemma of Margarete even more clearly: the spirits have said Faust should understand and grasp, but the rainbow cannot be grasped. Thus, the rainbow defines a more focused goal for Faust's striving in Part II: he must learn to create rainbows that can be both comprehended and literally grasped. This he does as he spends acts 1 through 3 conjuring a Helena whom he might embrace, then acts 4 and 5 creating a new community on land reclaimed from the sea.

The first three acts progress from grasping toward a heightened comprehension that allows for the synthesis of literal and figurative. During the masque in act 1, for example, the audience of Faust's play snatches in vain after the gifts of Boy-Charioteer and recoils in horror from Mephistopheles/Greed's equally unreal obscenities. Even the emperor mistakes the offering of Faust/ Plutus's gold as literal and reaches for it, setting fire to his beard and the entire hall. This is at least as catastrophic as Faust's taking physical possession of Margarete in Part I. Similarly, after the masque, and after the emperor has issued his paper money, he is appalled to discover that all of his subjects intend to continue their previous mindless lives of luxury. Only the mysteriously resuscitated fool will become a farmer and actually produce something. Thus no one at court—excepting, as always, the fool–has learned that banknotes, like plays, are representations that must be creatively translated by an audience into constructive activity. Grasped and treated as literal objects, they become horrors. Faust himself does little better when he tries to grasp the shade of Helena at the end of act 1 and she explodes in his face. Representations, aesthetic or otherwise, are categorically different from reality, and their autonomy must be respected.

Faust approaches the creations of the mind much more cautiously in acts 2 and 3. He spends an act and a half building an elaborate series of settings—mythic, historic, aesthetic, poetic—in which Helena can be comprehended one aspect at a time. When the two finally appear on stage together in act 3 he does not embrace her but modestly kisses her hand as she raises him to join her on a pedestal, where they sit like a pair of living statues. Characters who grasp only physically in these scenes have no success: Mephistopheles snatches at young beauties who dance around him in the *Classical Walpurgis Night,* and they turn into hags; Euphorion, son of Faust's and Helena's offstage embrace, seizes a maiden in the chorus, and she bursts into flame. Faust, by contrast, embraces Helena on stage only as she prepares to follow her son to the Underworld. She dissolves in his arms, but her clothing is transformed into a cloud that carries him off into the sky, deposits him in Germany at the beginning of act 4, and withdraws to the east as the distant inspiration of classical antiquity. Faust has fully comprehended Helena by entering into all aspects of her context and style without violating her autonomy. As a result the tragedy of Part I gives way to gentler, more abstract renunciation at the end of act 3.

NATURE, SOCIETY, AND ART

The world of Part II is clearly a much different place from that of Part I, not only because it is larger. The first scene sets the tone: kindly nature spirits heal Faust of his guilt from Part I; then this already-symbolic action is generalized in the celebration of the sunrise. There is no explanation for the presence of Faust or the elves, nor for the notable absence of Mephistopheles. The realistic details of Faust's healing are of equally little interest. Since the action has become entirely allegorical, matters of credibility and motivation can be dispensed with, and the issue is only what the action signifies. The world in Part II is understood automatically to represent higher truth to the audience, just as it does to Faust.

Nature is both the central actor and topic of this scene. It is first personified in the elves and Ariel, who is familiar not only from Shakespeare's *Tempest*, in which he changes form, sings, and executes Prospero's various theatricals, but also from the *Walpurgis Night's Dream*, in which he invites the audience at the end to escape to banks of roses. He is nature at its most theatrical. In the elfin song time moves from dusk to sunrise, so that the song has itself created the world it describes and caused the operatic sunrise accompanied by fanfares of trumpets and trombones. Similarly, Faust seems to create the brightening world around him as he describes it in the process of becoming. The creativity of nature looks remarkably like the creativity of the human mind; henceforth the play does not distinguish between nature and art as reflections of higher truth.

In the course of the first three acts, art generated out of the self definitively replaces nature as the locus of mediation. When nature appears it is generated by a creating voice, as, for example, when Faust generates the Arcadia in which he will live with Helena. All along, this subjectivity of knowledge has been a lurking problem for Faust. The special contribution of acts 1 through 3 is to define the historical range of the cultural tradition as the objective context in which subjective creation operates. As Faust goes to the Mothers, as he wanders among the alien yet familiar figures of the *Classical Walpurgis Night*, as he creates and enacts the phantasmagoria of his marriage to Helena through the history of European poetic style, he grounds his vision of the ideal in the reality of the cultural tradition. Indeed, Faust may be said to colonize the tradition, for at the end of *Inner Courtyard* he distributes the ancient sections of Greece among his German followers. Faust seeking Helena among the classical ghosts personifies the modern European mind, and more specifically the modern German mind, seeking possession of the classical tradition for itself. Faust's creativity here validates that tradition, to make it both accessible and meaningful for Goethe and his contemporaries. As Goethe justifies his own classicism and integrates modern Germany into the larger European tradition, it becomes difficult to draw the line between theories of creativity and cultural politics.

The implications of the shift from politics to aesthetics are manifold. The search for Helena originated, we recall, in a political problem in act 1, the stability of the impoverished empire. The three parallel modes of creation in the masque in act 1—poetic, social, and sexual—showed that one could readily represent the other, and the paper-money scheme, a political issue of contemporary importance, involves paper representing money. In his "Fairy Tale," written in 1795 in response to the French Revolution, Goethe had gone so far as to make appearance (*Schein* again) one of the three pillars of his utopian postrevolutionary state, along with wisdom and power. Thus, it is no longer a matter of an aesthetic issue representing a political issue; instead, politics itself is a matter of aesthetics.

The profundity of Goethe's analysis has often been overlooked by critics, who sometimes happily, sometimes angrily assume that Faust's descent into a world of art in Part II is an escape from the social problems of the emperor's court and of Goethe's own day. But as we have seen, the representational nature of even material social institutions like money makes the political problem an aesthetic problem. In both cases in the first half of Part II, the problem is the autonomy of the work of art, or, more generally, of the representation. No representational object can be directly appropriated—"grasped." Representations so treated may turn into insects, disappear, or even explode. In this view, Faust's long detour to establish the historical validity of his Helena also represents a change in his relation to the admired aesthetic object, whose individual context and historical uniqueness are developed at great length. It is the paradox of dialectics that Faust gains access to Helena by recognizing and reenacting her difference from himself and thereby respecting her autonomy. She can be for him not a permanent wife but an abiding and inspiring memory at a distance that will provoke him to new deeds. Similarly, the courtiers in act 1 were wrong to spend the paper money as they had their gold money on consumerist luxuries; they should have, like the fool, invested in land or other enterprises to stimulate new productivity—in effect, used it as inspiration—in what might well have been called a capitalist aesthetic.

In both the social and aesthetic spheres, then, representations can only be usefully appropriated or grasped by being internalized and made the source of inspiration for creative activity by the user or viewer. The role of the receiver in the act of reception or interpretation thus becomes central to our understanding of the creative process and of the social process. Neither institutions nor works of art change the world simply by virtue of existing: *Faust* demonstrates this truth repeatedly with its weak emperor, ineffective monetary pranks, the court in flames from the gold of Plutus in the masque, the insects of Boy-Charioteer, the explosive shade of Helena, and even the glorious dream of Faust's marriage to Helena, which dissolves back into nature and leaves Mephistopheles once again in control of the world. Yet Panthalis, leader of Helena's maidens, raises herself to permanence by her response to the play, the emperor's jester becomes a landowner, and Faust carries off the memory of Helena—they are all stronger and richer as the result of art. During the height of his work on Part II, in 1827, Goethe wrote in an essay entitled "On Didactic Poetry," "All poetry should teach, but unnoticeably; it should make people notice where something could be learned; they have to do the learning from it, as from life, by themselves."[8] In this respect it hardly matters whether Faust's experience with Helena was a dream, as some critics argue, or "real" (whatever that means in this play), or a play-within-the-play. Only what Faust carries off from it has lasting significance.

Since change comes only from the creative work of the viewer to change herself or himself or to carry something with her or him in response to an institution or to the work of art, Goethe's social and aesthetic thought alike are grounded in the creativity of the thoughtful and well-trained individual. In the 1790s he and Schiller had used their journals and the Weimar stage as a forum to develop a coherent program of *Bildung*, as they called this theory of a social order based on educated individuals; by the 1820s it was long since obvious to Goethe how utopian such a program was. In *Faust: Part II* this creative activity is carried on only by individuals; it does not generate a stable social order. It is the ideal, or Faustian, pole opposing Mephistopheles' chaotic reality.

9

Part II: The Outer Perspective

The second half of Part II returns the drama to the Mephistophelean perspective on the world and to its normal tension with the
Faustian view. At the beginning of act 4 Helena's cloud drops Faust
at the top of a mountain range then recedes eastward, while Faust
notices a wisp of grey cloud that remains nearby and represents
Margarete: the descents are over, and Faust has returned to the
German north. Here Mephistopheles counters Faust's play of
Helena with military and political shows designed to engage Faust
once again in the real world. If the first half of Part II explored the
classical ideal in European culture, the second explores a modern
world stripped of that ideal. Now the epistemological significance of
nature has retreated, comprehending has been succeeded by
piracy, and permanence has become temporality. At the end of act
5 Faust dies and is carried off to Heaven. It remains to be seen
what that might mean, and whether and how that might be understood from the Mephistophelean perspective.

DEMYTHOLOGIZED NATURE

In the first half of Part II nature readily represented the ideal in the
world. It was the equivalent of art; indeed, it was art, called into
being at the word of elves and of Faust, and in the myths of antiq-

uity. The watery landscapes of acts 2 and 3, as well as the Arcadia of act 3, were not real but the projections of ancient myths and poems. Everywhere in act 2, whether by the water or in the mountains, the landscape came alive and spoke through the voices of resident nymphs, gods, or personifications (figures of art), until the entire phenomenon was condensed into the one figure of Galatea, who personified both nature and art simultaneously. But in act 4 the watery landscapes of Greek mythology give way to the fires, volcanos, and noxious gases of Mephistopheles' demonology. The masque of Seismos in act 2 discredited the creative power of fire, but now Mephistopheles restores it to honor with the Christian myth that the mountains were forced up by the fallen angels after they landed in Hell. This nature is more violent and dangerous, and it is controlled by Christian myth, by Milton's *Paradise Lost* and the Bible.

Nevertheless, it is difficult to take Mephistopheles' mythology quite so seriously as the mythology of the *Classical Walpurgis Night*, because the description of all the devils coughing in Hell to create mountains (10081–88) and all the biblical quotations Mephistopheles drops (explicitly identified in the text) sound like parody. When Mephistopheles offers Faust "the realms of the world and their glories" (10131), echoing Satan's offer to Jesus (Matthew 4:8), Faust, unlike Jesus, accepts the devil's offer. The fact that Homunculus had rejected the equivalent offer of Seismos's mountain with all its wealth in act 2 enhances the sense of parody. Mephistopheles' victory over the counter-emperor's army with ghostly flames and phantom water rushing down the mountainsides reveals his mythology of nature to be pure stage managing—decoration and nothing more.

Faust entirely ignores Mephistopheles' parodistic mythology. He regards this mountainscape neither with the terror Mephistopheles would like nor with the reverence of act 2. Instead, he says, "Mountain masses remain nobly silent, / I ask neither whence nor why. / As Nature developed of itself, / It rounded the earthly sphere off smooth" (10095–98). This nature, existing in itself, created by itself to no purpose outside of itself, is not the emotionally charged carrier of truth Faust wanted nature to be in Part I, nor is it the calmer but still divinely haunted mythological nature Faust just left. It is instead contemporary nature. Writers like Schiller and Heine in Germany, and Wordsworth in England, from the 1790s through the early decades of the nineteenth century, lamented the disappearance of the classical divinities from nature. At the moment, Faust does not need nature to represent anything.

But Faust is not one to let things be themselves for long: the less nature is needed to satisfy Faust's epistemological demands, the more it becomes an object of his activity. "Deed" was his final translation for *logos* in the Bible translation scene (1237), and now it becomes the most consistent expression for his eternal striving. Here he accepts the barren seashore from Mephistopheles, in order to drain the land and build dikes to keep out the sea. If act 3 brought the drama into the age of contemporary literature, act 4 brings it into the age of contemporary technology, for drainage and reclamation projects had been gaining momentum in the Netherlands and North Germany since the late sixteenth century. Faust will not trouble silent nature for its secrets, but he will attempt to control it and make use of it. Nature is no longer the object of reverent knowledge, but of technological exploitation as everything in the play, including Faust's striving, is seen from the Mephistophelean perspective.

The shift in perspective makes all of the markers of Faust's striving reverse. In act 2 both Faust's and Homunculus' quests for form led them to the water—to the visions of Leda and the swan among the reeds, to Helen at the beginning of act 3 on the reedy banks of the Eurotas, to Galatea gliding on her shell-chariot. Homunculus renounced the mountain created by fire to descend to the sea. Even in *Charming Landscape* Faust turned away from the fire of the rising sun to view the rainbow in the droplets of water behind him. But now in act 4 Faust turns against the water that act 2 celebrated as the source of all life and attacks it as sterile. Faust may be wrong here as he adopts Mephistopheles' denying stance, but "Man errs as long as he strives" (317), as the Lord said long since in the *Prologue in Heaven.* Faust has learned that his striving must be directed into the world; nevertheless, all action in the world is doomed to error—otherwise the world would not be the world but the ideal. In the Christian terms with which the beginning of act 4 plays, nature is fallen since the Fall of Lucifer, and therefore action in the world is inevitably sinful. Faust's negative attitude toward the water shares in the tragedy innate in the human condition.

PIRACY

The new project leads immediately to ethical error. No sooner has Faust determined to drive back the sea than he learns that Mephistopheles intends to exploit the coming war between our old friend the emperor and an upstart rival to win Faust the right to the seashore. War is already dubious enough to Faust, but Mephistopheles' three mighty men, who will remain Faust's servants into act 5, are much more so. The stage direction after line 10322 refers to the Book of Samuel, which describes the devotion of his three greatest heroes to King David, himself a king prone to error. Their names, Bully, Snatch, and Holdfast, speak for themselves: they are graspers in the literal sense. Faust's conquest of the sea is thus not only anti-water but also on the wrong side of the opposition between comprehension and literal grasping.

Most of Faust's activity in the last two acts can be understood in this context. The battle between the two emperors determines which will hold (grasp) power; Faust exploits the battle to take possession of the seashore. Act 5 shows the aged Faust still in the company of his three mighty men, whose commercial voyages are indistinguishable from piracy. At home his drainage projects have enabled him to establish new settlements on former swamps. But like many colonial rulers, in the interest of consolidating his domains, he allows his three mighty men to relocate—and in the process accidentally massacre—the less-developed natives (in this case the elderly Baucis and Philemon). This is the grasping that destroyed Margarete, generalized to the level of society. Goethe identifies the fundamental economic and political aspirations of the nineteenth century, commerce and colonialism as piracy at bottom—the violence of the strong against the weak.

The new ascendancy of grasping in this part of the play forces us to reconsider all the grasping in Part II from the Mephistophelean perspective. The paper-money scheme in act 1 is obviously a sophisticated form of theft, though the victim would only be identifiable when the system collapsed and someone was left holding worthless paper. Even in the long aesthetic interlude of acts 2 and 3, in which grasping is mainly figurative comprehension, there are innumerable examples of less-elevated grasping. Mephistopheles, for example, begins his quest with the griffins, whose pride is holding fast, and the sphinxes, whose claws the devil admires; both names are etymologically related to grasping. Seismos's mountain becomes the home of greed in action as ants dig gold from its crevices, first for the griffins to guard, then for the dactyls (the name means fingers, also necessary for grasping), who are in turn enslaved by the murderous pygmies. Although Homunculus wisely rejects the offer of empire over these greedy folk, he himself plays the role of Zeus raping Leda in the water when he breaks his vial and his flame flows into the water all around Galatea. Helena herself is another woman at the mercy of whoever can grasp her—whether Theseus, the pirate Menelaus, Paris, Achilles (Mephistopheles/Phorcyas recites the list in lines 8848–80), or Faust. Lynceus arranges all the treasure in Faust's castle—he and his men have stolen much booty as they have colonized Greece—to greet Helena, largely because she herself is another stolen treasure. Small wonder that Euphorion's birth closely imitates that of Hermes, whose epithet was Lord of Robbers. Euphorion rapidly grows up to imitate what both his father and Mephistopheles have been up to—snatching at pretty girls. As we have also seen, Goethe himself borrowed freely from the entire Western tradition, especially in this section of the play. Even—or perhaps especially—the poet in this play is a thief.

Staggering as the extent and range of the thievery is, once it is collected together like this, it lacks the negative impact of the fewer but nastier examples of grasping in acts 4 and 5. The difference is again one of perspective. If the last two acts reveal the worldly, conventional perspective that grasping is evil, the second and third show the idealist perspective that it is a form of creativity or higher understanding. After all, gold—the object of theft, like fire, light, and Helen—tends to represent the ineffable truth that cannot be perceived directly; it should certainly be comprehended, if not grasped.

The hints in act 3 that even the poet is a thief illustrate the ambiguity of this dialectic most clearly. In the myth of Hermes, partly recounted by the chorus (9645–78), the god of thieves invents the lyre and escapes the consequences of his first theft by giving it to Apollo, god of poetry. There exists a wise god who steals, who patronizes thieves, and who contributes to the poet's art. Goethe's extensive use of allusions and imitations of other writers, especially in act 3, is analogous—it could be narrowly understood as a kind of theft, plagiarism, but is also the basis of Goethe's creativity. Act 3 suggests that modern poetry must ground itself in a previous poetic tradition to keep from being entirely subjective or solipsistic. The ambiguity is particularly pressing for Goethe. Until the mid-eighteenth century authors expected to treat plots, characters, themes, and often ideas that had been treated many times before. Only after the 1750s did an aesthetic of original genius begin to be discussed; it took hold rapidly in the seventies as young writers in Germany, Goethe foremost among them, proclaimed it as doctrine. Perhaps no single idea separates romanticism more emphatically from what came before than original genius. In his old age Goethe thus defends an aesthetic of convention, which he himself had not only attacked but had virtually destroyed. The imagery of theft transforms use of the literary tradition from an aesthetic to a moral issue. Thus, Goethe's ambivalent position on it in Part II reveals the network connecting the temporal dialectic of classical and modern with the ethical issues at the heart of *Faust*.

TEMPORALITY

Time, too, seems to have changed in the last two acts of the play. It is not just that the play has returned from a timeless aesthetic world to the temporal world but that time has become even more important during Faust's absence. Suddenly the play is full of old people—Baucis and Philemon, Faust himself—and full of memories and losses. The pressure of time in the last act has the same effect as the theme of piracy in revealing an implicit pressure of time during the whole period that the play seemed to be out of time altogether.

It is most clearly visible at the end of Faust's quest for Helena in the *Classical Walpurgis Night.* Chiron brings Faust to the eternal temple of Manto, daughter of Aesculapius (god of healing), who will lead Faust to Persephone, and they exchange the following words:

MANTO: Do you still wander tirelessly?
CHIRON: You still dwell surrounded by peace,
             While I take pleasure in circling.
MANTO: I wait, Time circles me. (7478–81)

Manto represents the timeless realm to which Faust is about to escape, while Chiron, the circler, seems to represent temporality itself. If temporality is what encircles Manto, it can be defined more precisely. Chiron describes the location of her temple with, "Here Rome and Greece stood opposed in battle, / Peneius to the right, Olympus to the left side, / The greatest of empires, that runs dry in the sand; The king flees, citizens triumph" (7465–68). The setting is the fields of Pharsalus, the battlefield where the Roman republic met its end: temporality consists of war and revolution. Seismos's mountain, from which Homunculus fled to the sea and from which even Mephistopheles fled to the natural mountain cave of the Phorcyads, was a place of war and oppression. Erichtho, the witch who speaks the prologue to the *Classical Walpurgis Night,* describes the setting in terms of constant battles and civil strife. The temporality that swirls around Manto's entrance to the underworld of forms is war and social violence.

Once the connection is made, it becomes evident that violence and war have always been the implicit background. In act 1 the play moved toward art and away from the instability of the empire. In Part I, in *Before the City Gate,* the first topic of conversation among the citizens on Easter morning was the war in Turkey, while the pact with the devil was to plunge Faust into the "rushing of time" (1754). Even the archangels' hymn in the *Prologue in Heaven* devoted an entire stanza to the stormy violence of nature (259–66). But in Part II the pattern becomes particularly intense. Faust escapes the political anxieties of the court by descending to the silent realm of the Mothers; then he departs from the "whirlpool" (7483) of the *Classical Walpurgis Night* to the silent realm of the dead. All through act 3 the aesthetic zone in which he can encounter Helena is surrounded, threatened, and indeed defined by the clamor of history just outside. Helena has supposedly just returned from the Trojan War. Her husband, Menelaus, is about to sacrifice her and murder all her women. Menelaus is about to attack the fortress in which Faust greets Helena. The marriage of Faust and Helena is consummated, and their son is born deep in a cave protected by a shady grove within an Arcadia beyond whose rocky walls war rages. Euphorion responds to the call of the war outside as he climbs to his death, and once the idyll has come to an end, Faust too returns to a world at war.

That the temporal world is Mephistopheles' realm and is therefore a place of chaos and violence is a familiar idea. What is new, or at least much more explicit in Part II, is that its antithesis is no longer the permanent transcendent realm of the ideal, but art. Acts 2 and 3 show Faust withdrawing into an aesthetic realm essentially of his own imagining, though validated by its connection to a historical tradition outside of himself. The situation is clear in the allegory of Homunculus, who is enclosed in his crystal vial because he is artificial. Goethe opposes art to a world at war in his autobiographical works from the same decade as *Faust: Part II*. The best example is *Campaign in France* (1822), in which Goethe recounts his participation in the Allied campaign against the French in 1792. The Allies marched into France with little resistance, but after a disastrous defeat at Valmy, they fled home in disarray (and in pouring rain), with supply lines cut and disease among the troops. Goethe concludes his narrative by describing a visit to friends in the Rhineland, where they discussed not the exciting political events of the day but antique carved gems, which he even borrowed to take home to Weimar. The healing alternative to the violence of history is withdrawal into art, just as in *Faust*. Such withdrawal is not escapism but a time of gathering; the following summer Goethe returned to the wars to lay siege, successfully this time, to the city of Mainz. Such oscillation between war and art, or between politics and art, had to be typical for any intellectual living in Europe during the Napoleonic Wars; neither Goethe nor Faust is an exception.

But the crass opposition between the aesthetic Faust who marries Helena and the political Faust in whose service Baucis and

Philemon are murdered makes resolution of the opposition between art and temporality particularly pressing. How can the impassioned seeker after the classical heritage allow the destruction of the elderly couple who, after all, also come to us from classical mythology? The contrast seems even worse because of Faust's watchman Lynceus, who describes both the spectacular arrival of Helena at the fortress (like the sun rising in the south) in act 3 (9224–25) and the similar bright light, this time fire, that accompanies the destruction of Baucis and Philemon in act 5 (11307–35). Lynceus functions as Faust's eye for classical antiquity, and he eloquently voices the admiration for it of later generations, who are embodied in Faust. When, in *Deep Night*, Lynceus first celebrates "the eternal pattern" (11297), then ends his mourning for Baucis and Philemon with "What once appealed to the eye, / Is gone with the centuries" (11336–37), he registers the destruction of the classical ideal.

If, however, the classical ideal can be destroyed, then antiquity itself is subject to time. Galatea is the historical successor, a late version, of the goddess Venus. She appears in act 2 (after line 8423) at the end of a long pageant of mythological figures who enter the play in roughly chronological order, starting with the griffins and sphinxes, who belong to the oldest levels of classical mythology. Act 3, similarly, is structured as a historical progression, this time of literary forms. The idea that classical culture is not a timeless ideal but has a history and internal development was new in the eighteenth century, for the first real history of ancient art had only been published in 1764 by Johann Joachim Winckelmann (*History of Ancient Art*), whom Goethe very much admired. Baucis and Philemon are the last classical figures to appear in *Faust*. Theirs is a late myth, first appearing in Ovid's *Metamorphoses*, at the end of the classical age. The elderly couple is the only family in the village to welcome the disguised Jupiter and Mercury, who have come to see if men still honor the gods. When the village is transformed into a swamp for its lack of hospitality to travelers, Baucis and Philemon are made guardians of a small temple and finally turned into trees because they are too old to live any more. Thus, they come from a very late stage in classical literature, they are themselves very elderly, and their story is about a late age: they are the classical ideal grown very old.

Insofar as the ideal is represented in the world, that representation is subject to time, like anything else. Thus, no representation that we can call an ideal can last forever, even the very literary tradition to which we anchor our subjectivity to make it objective. At the end of Part II the ideal appears in the form of the "eternal feminine" (12110), as Faust floats upward led by Margarete toward the form of the Holy Virgin. But the Holy Virgin is also floating upward ahead of Faust, constantly receding from both his grasp and his comprehension. It became typical in the nineteenth century to represent the afterlife as a blissful continuation of life itself, and Goethe is a pioneer in that trend,[9] for Faust's striving, his upward movement toward the ideal, will apparently continue in all eternity. Striving, purposive movement through and with time in all eternity is the essence of salvation and the resolution of the temporal dialectic in the play. Goethe has historicized not only the classical ideal but eternity as well.

THE DEATH OF FAUST

All of the central themes in the play come together in the scenes that immediately precede Faust's death. Having in effect murdered Baucis and Philemon in his haste to add their little plot to his vast domains, Faust faces the allegorical figure of Care, who alone of her siblings can gain access to him. It appears that Faust pulls himself together in this confrontation, repents his use of the devil's magic, renounces it, and is, as a result, saved. If this were the case, Goethe would, so to speak, have reversed all the patterns on which the play has insisted. What really happens is more complex and more interesting.

Care is the first problem in these scenes. Who is she, and why can she come to Faust when Want, Misery, and Debt (or Guilt—the German word *Schuld* means both) cannot? Faust's pact with Mephistopheles evidently protects him from all material need and, as we have seen, from conventional social guilt as well. Care, however, is used in a much broader sense. Even in Part I Faust refers in passing (644–51) to Care as what disrupts one's relationship to the world. Now, in act 5, Care says explicitly, "For him whom I once possess, / The whole world is of no use" (11453–54). Her victim becomes so anxious about the future that he loses all sense of time and can no longer experience the world. Thus Care blocks striving, for a person who cannot experience the world cannot seek the higher truth represented by it. Faust thus confirms his striving, the essence of his humanity, when he refuses to acknowledge Care.

Yet his great speech in opposition to Care is famous as his renunciation of magic and of transcendent knowledge. He justifies his refusal to exorcise this phantom with a magic word by saying,

> I have always rushed through the world;
> Every pleasure I seized by the hair,
> What did not suffice I dropped,
> What escaped me I let go.
> I have only demanded and only completed
> And again desired and so with might
> Stormed through my life; once grandly and mightily,
> But now I go wisely, go calmly. (11433–40)

All through the play Faust has been trying to gain possession of as much time as possible, just as he has been trying to experience as much of the world as possible. Mephistopheles' magic, we saw, was a shortcut for Faust to use his time as efficiently as possible. Now the deaths of Baucis and Philemon force him to realize that he is again grasping and erring. In this respect, Faust embodies the modern age. In his last novel, *Wilhelm Meister's Journeyman Years*, Goethe laments the increasingly rapid pace of life brought on by the industrial revolution. Time itself has speeded up, and the consequences for human life are seen in the grimmest terms.

Faust reacts to the increased pressure of modern time not by seeking escape into permanence but by forcing himself to slow down and move at a natural pace, to "go wisely" and "calmly." The continuation of this same speech elaborates the implications of such patience with nature.

> The circle of the world is sufficiently familiar,
> The view into the beyond is blocked;
> Fool, who strains his eyes to see so far,
> Inventing his like above the clouds!
> Let him stand fast and look about him here;
> To the capable man the world is not silent.

Why does he need to roam around eternity!
What he comprehends he can seize.
Let him thus proceed along the earthly day;
If spirits come spooking, let him continue on his way,
In marching on may he find torment and joy,
Unsatisfied every moment! (11441–52)

Faust now firmly rejects the idea that his striving should be for a transcendent goal above him and out of the world. He should not seek his like above the clouds—remember his distress when the earth spirit insisted Faust was not his like (514)—but hear the voice of the world. He affirms that access to truth, what the Bible called the *logos*, is through deeds in the world, not through transcendence. Thus, when Care blinds him she does not reverse the development of the play but completes it: Faust can and will continue to act in the world through Mephistopheles and his followers, spirits of the world. And indeed, Faust's inner light shines all the brighter after he is blinded. The entire thrust of the play has been to show that the human mind cannot perceive a light shining from outside and above the world, only its reflections in the world, in the rainbow and in the plays that the mind itself creates.

Now, therefore, the thematics of word returns to the play in new form. At the beginning of Part I Faust rejected words and "word-mongering" as inadequate forms of knowledge; he could not allow the *logos* to be a word, so he translated it as "deed." But now at the end of Part II, after the words of the spirits have brought the new day in *Pleasant Landscape* and after Faust has created Arcadia with his own words, the word has been restored to a position of respect. Above all, Faust wants to guard himself from saying a "magic word" (11423) to drive Care away, and after she has blinded him, he says, "The night seems to press in deeper and deeper, / But inside me shines bright light; / What I conceived I'll hasten to complete; / The master's *word*, it alone has weight" (11499–502, emphasis mine). In a typical dialectical move Faust has to reject the word in order to possess it fully. The play thus comes full circle: Faust began by rejecting knowledge of the world and of the word for a higher truth, and now sees that higher truth, the shining bright light, is in the world and in the very words that he rejected. If the project of the *Classical Walpurgis Night* was to revalidate the classical tradition, that of the play as a whole is to revalidate the poetic word, to restore to it the mythological power of the creating *logos* after the fall of Western Europe into rational scientific knowledge.

At this point there is nothing left for Faust to do; Goethe and the audience are satisfied, even if Faust is not. Having just revalidated the word, Goethe must perforce return to the terms of the wager, which depended on Faust speaking the particular words he so carefully avoided at the end of Part I: "Tarry a while, thou art so fair!" At line 11582 he speaks them and adds for good measure, "Now I enjoy the highest moment" (11586). He does not lose the bet and can be saved because he speaks the words only "in anticipation" (11585) of the time when his great project, draining the swamps and seeing a community "of free people on free soil" (11580) daily reconquer its living space from the dangerous forces of nature, should be completed. The project is certainly not completed when Faust says the words; it is his dream, another of his creative plays-within-the-play and, as such, the only highest moment attainable in the world.

Mephistopheles, as usual, expresses a different point of view, and with it the Faustian synthesis unravels, as it always must. Mephistopheles calls Faust's highest moment "the last, lousy, empty moment" (11589). "It is," he says, "as good as if it had never been" (11601), and he is entirely correct. Faust's great triumph, his "every-thing," is only an illusion, Mephistopheles' "nothing." It is important neither to overestimate nor to underestimate the significance of his commentary. Faust's illusion of a final synthesis is only an illusion, and the autonomy of the representation must be respected. But the significance of illusion has been established too firmly by the rest of the play for Mephistopheles' denial to render Faust's insight valueless. Instead, we are still in the play's pattern of alternating synthesis and dissolution. As Faust follows his eternally receding ideal in the final scene, this alternation will be played out forever, just as birth and death will always succeed one another in the eternal order of nature.

Yet the sympathetic treatment given to Mephistopheles raises important questions about Faust's synthesis. That his great project involves the murder of Baucis and Philemon, human sacrifices (suggested by Baucis in line 11127), lands earned in a war won by trickery, and riches earned by piracy disturbs us anew as the ghostly lemurs dig not a ditch but Faust's grave, and as unbearably attractive angels seize Faust's soul from the jaws of Hell by arousing the fires of homosexual love in Mephistopheles himself. The devil is offered love objects, just as he offered Margarete and Helena to Faust. The fact that the methods of Heaven are no different from those of Hell is part of Faust's—or is it Goethe's?—great synthesis, but it intensifies rather than stills our moral qualms.

The eternal order of nature, with its inevitable alternation of day and night, may make sense to the eye that views it from above and outside, as the archangels do in the *Prologue in Heaven*, and as Faust learns to do. But to experience it from within like Baucis and Philemon, or like Margarete in Part I, is painful, to say the least. Even Mephistopheles suffers the trials of Job (11809), absurdly enough, at the hands of an inscrutable Providence. Everything involved in saving Faust seems desperately unfair. Within the world, affairs appear in the Mephistophelean perspective: there is injustice, disorder, evil, and innocent suffering, and they are really there. Baucis and Philemon really are destroyed by brute force; Faust's drive for constructive activity in the world does go grievously astray. Yet as long as Faust accepts the burden of his humanity, to live in time and to change with it, a Baucis who cleaves to her heritage, a Margarete who wants to relive the past, a Mephistopheles who wants to hold on to the old version of the Faust story will be destroyed—if not by Faust, then by the cosmos itself.

Completely moral action is impossible for Goethe, because it would require operating simultaneously in terms of the eternal order of heaven and the temporal order of the world. *Faust* thus makes us painfully aware of the amorality of the cosmos. Goethe sums up this situation in aphorisms that he wrote and collected in his later years; for example, "One always acts without conscience; only the observer has a conscience."[10] What could more accurately describe Faust than this:

> All of life consists of
> Wanting and not achieving,
> Achieving and not wanting.[11]

Given its general application, Faust's tricky salvation does not "justify" Faustian striving; it does not validate either wanton or considered destruction of those around one to achieve higher goals, whatever they may be, as many nationalist readers wanted it to. It is, rather, profoundly realistic because it confronts all of us with the inevitable gap between thought and action, between eternal order and life in the world.

THE FINAL "SYNTHESIS"

The last scene of the play does little to heal this gap. After almost 12,000 lines of league with the devil, of undermining the biblical definition of sin and ordinary ethics and religious values, of hostility to organized religion, the great burst of Catholic baroque imagery can hardly convince us that all moral concerns can be laid to rest. The image of the Virgin floating upward through a mountainous landscape inhabited by hermits praising nature and divinity is familiar from seventeenth-century paintings of the Assumption of the Virgin (the rising of the Virgin Mary to Heaven) but is clearly somewhat ironic here. At a minimum, it is peculiar to place Faust, the seducer of Margarete (whose spirit now leads him!) in the context of the apotheosis of the Virgin. In fact, we have a double apotheosis, of the Virgin and of the seducer—representing both perspectives in the play. That Faust will apparently continue to float upward eternally, following his ever receding ideal, also shows there can be no real resolution here.

The final mystical chorus reiterates in completely abstract terms that this obviously stagy ending is the only resolution the play can ever have:

> Everything transient
> Is only a likeness;
> What cannot be achieved,
> Here comes to pass;
> The indescribable,
> Here it's enacted;
> The eternal feminine
> Draws us on. (12104–11)

For the last time Goethe insists that we see before us "only a likeness," a representation of what is ineffable and indescribable. In this temporary likeness, enacted on stage, in the world, the ineffable principle represented in the phrase "eternal feminine" draws us toward itself—but only "toward," not "to." Neither we nor Faust will ever reach it; we will all remain ever strivers, for such is the human condition.

The play remains open in all the different categories that could be used to describe it, or in terms of all the different issues that have been raised. Faust has learned but been blinded, will always strive after the higher truth now embodied in the Virgin but never reach it, remains a piratical grasper but is saved, is permanent but ever changing. Similarly, the play itself is a tragedy (the goal cannot ever be reached) but has a happy ending (the hero is saved), as it both ends and does not end.

To understand why Goethe would end his masterpiece so ambiguously after some 12,000 lines of text (*Faust* is three times the length of *Hamlet*), it helps to consider his ideas about development. Goethe's central interest in the field of biology was development, both within an organism, as in the development of a plant from seed to stem to leaf to flower, and between species. In plants, for example, he tried to demonstrate how all the different organs—leaf, petal, stamen, root—develop in increasingly specialized ways from one fundamental protoform in the seed. He searched for and discovered the intermaxillary bone in man because all lower mammals have it, and he believed firmly that the continuity of development in animal species must imply its presence in man as well. In all cases continuity dominated his thinking.

Nevertheless, Goethe was a fundamentally dialectical thinker, so that the language he most often used to describe development was "polarity and heightening" ("Polarität und Steigerung"), which is not far from the more traditional "opposition and synthesis." Hegel and Schiller called synthesis "sublimation," which is even closer to "heightening." But "polarity" or "opposition" imply constant division, which does not seem to fit with continuity. To unite these opposed structures in his thought, Goethe tended to visualize development as a spiral curve, which is continuous and moves ever upward, yet when seen in two dimensions appears to move back and forth between two poles. It is also, and this is very important for Goethe, open: it can be continued indefinitely, circling ever onward. Since representations are so important in *Faust*, it is not surprising that such an image is central to Goethe's way of knowing even in the scientific arena.

Once we understand how important the spiral was as a model of development for Goethe, the open ending of *Faust* is easier to understand. Closure would be death, the end of the spiral. But it would be death not to the individual but to the whole order of nature, for all life is part of one continuous spiral of development. Faust's upward movement at the end, with a cloud of unborn boys circling around him, is, in its combination of linear and circular movement, the line of nature. It is no longer the story of Faust that is being enacted, but the story of the entire cosmos. Whether we accept the triumphant tone of the final scene and affirm the natural order or whether we read it as an ironic and cynical assertion of the illusoriness of order depends on whether the Faustian or the Mephistophelean soul is stronger in us—for the play, as representation, is an analogue of that order which we can only perceive in our own mind's projection of it as interpretation.

10

Final Reflections: Imagery and Allusion

In *Elective Affinities*, a novel of 1809, Goethe mentions the ropes used by the British Navy, each of which had a single red thread woven through it to identify its owner; so too, he says, a certain characteristic way of looking at things ran all through his heroine's apparently disparate diary entries and revealed their author. This analogy is the model for the reading of *Faust* I have offered in this book. By exploiting the characteristic perspectives and dialectics in *Faust* as "red threads," I have been trying not only to pattern and unify a large and disparate work but also to go beyond patterning to suggest how the work responds to and helps to shape its social and historical context.

More commonly, Goethe's analogy of the red thread is associated with identifying patterns of imagery and interpreting their significance. An honorable tradition of such reading dates back to Shakespeare criticism in the early 1930s; it was extended by the New Criticism to all poetry and drama, finally to the novel, and even to *Faust*. It is sometimes derided as old-fashioned today, because its practitioners often did not show how such imagery affected either the statement made by the text or the relation of the text to anything else. We have, however, already identified in the various dialectics patterns more historically specific than imagery. If we now consider the relationship of the imagery to these dialectics, we will transcend the limits of formal description. Thus, a brief survey of some major images will help us to end with an effective overview of *Faust*.

Identifying allusions, references, and sources for particular figures and scenes in *Faust* is another "old-fashioned" method of reading that dates back even further, to the beginnings of modern literary scholarship in the mid-nineteenth century. As a method of commentary it succeeded in burying the text under so much information that it came to seem hopelessly esoteric and difficult, especially in Part II. If, however, one looks for patterns of allusions, as there are patterns of imagery and patterns of thinking in the play, then they too emerge as ways in which Goethe reflects on the place of *Faust* in history and tries to shape the course of Germany's and Europe's development.

LIGHT

The first words of the *Prologue in Heaven*, "The sun," establish light as the play's dominant image for the ineffable ideal. When the archangels say that gazing at it strengthens them, though they cannot fathom it, they join a tradition extending from the biblical prophets and Greek mythology: that the light of divine glory is too bright for human eyes to bear. Consistently in the play the sun represents the ideal. Faust wants to follow the sun forever in his speech to the sunset at the end of *Before the City Gate*; he must turn from the rising sun in *Charming Landscape* so as not to be blinded; Helena rises like the sun before the watchman Lynceus in act 3. In each case the image combines the glory and inaccessibility of divinity.

Darkness, by contrast, is associated with lack of divinity. Faust's narrow cell is dark and has dirty windows; Mephistopheles first approaches him at sunset. The places to which Mephistopheles leads Faust tend to be cavernous spaces lit by flickering lights—Auerbach's Cellar, the witch's kitchen, the cave in *Forest and Cavern*, the Walpurgis Night festivities, the realm of the Mothers, the halls of the emperor's court. Even Margarete's room, the first time Faust enters it, is in twilight. The world is dark where it is not lit by the sun of spirit.

Nevertheless, it is remarkable how many of these scenes in the world are lit by moonlight. Faust's first attempt to transcend the limits of his prison comes in a speech to the moon, the set of *Forest and Cavern* is bathed in moonlight, and the moon figures importantly in the *Classical Walpurgis Night*, both to end the war on Seismos's mountain and to light the final epiphany of Galatea. The moon also, like the sun, enlightens and orders. It is, however, more accessible than the sun: it is possible to look at the moon directly, for it shines only by reflected light. Because it mediates between the sun and the feeble eyes of man it is associated with art and representation. This is clearly its importance in the *Classical Walpurgis Night*, where the sirens even comment that the moon "shines double" (i.e., is reflected in the water [7513]) as they invite everyone to the shores where Galatea will appear. The *Prelude in the Theater* ties the sun to the moon when the director calls for the coming play to use "the great and small lights of heaven" (235). The moon is both a reflected and (as in *Forest and Cavern*) a reflective light, and in this sense an image for all images in the play.

Not only the sun and moon shine in the play. In Act I of Part II gold replaces the sun to represent the creative force and to be the object of striving. It accrues this significance only gradually and inconspicuously in the course of Part I. When Margarete sings about the King of Thule with his golden cup, and when Mephistopheles brings Margarete golden jewelry, nothing seems out of the ordinary. But when Margarete cries at the end of the same scene (*Evening*), "For gold all struggle, / On gold all depend. / Alas, poor us!" (2802–4) the tone is so different, so unexpected, that gold suddenly becomes more interesting and dangerous. The same thing happens when Faust sees the mountainside lit up by subterranean gold as he climbs the mountain on Walpurgis Night (3913–33). Mephistopheles explains that Mammon, devil of wealth, has decorated for the festival, but Faust describes the phenomenon in such beautiful, delicate, and natural terms that like the rest of the *Walpurgis Night*, it does not seem the conventional temptation of evil. We are prepared, then, for the ambiguity of gold in Part II, where it can both save and destroy the state, generate both new life and war. Boy-Charioteer strews ephemeral treasure about in act 1; in act 3 Helena becomes a treasure to be grasped like the gold and jewels that Faust's men have already amassed; and in acts 4 and 5 the three mighty men continue to steal and amass treasure. Gold can be fashioned into constructive representations or guarantors of higher order, such as money, but it can also promote the most brutal disorder. Being of the world, it is a much more ambiguous symbol than the sun.

Light imagery in the play could be pursued much further, but we have seen enough to understand some of the issues. The sun might be described as a symbol—one thing that represents something else with some consistency. But it also proliferates through the play in forms that become more fluid as they move farther from the source. Gold becomes both literally fluid in act 1, and also more ambiguous and more subject to manipulation. Yet it can still stand in for the sun on occasion, particularly in act 1. This tendency for an image to proliferate is one important aspect of the red threads that unify *Faust.*

DRINKING

A tradition going back to the Roman historian Tacitus makes the Germans the heaviest drinkers in Europe. Perhaps the importance of drinking in *Faust* was one way Goethe wanted to make the play specifically German. But drinking also has serious implications, which first appear in the *Prelude in the Theater,* in which the harlequin describes the play itself as a drink: "In varied images a little clarity, / Much error and a spark of truth, / Thus is brewed the best drink, / That refreshes and edifies the whole world" (170–73). The harlequin mediates here between the confusion promoted by the director and the clarity of the poet. Since the director only wants to give his audience a lot to see, and the poet only wants only to hear eternal harmonies, they embody opposing modes of perception, as well as opposing modes of everything else. The drink offered by the harlequin is to be neither seen nor heard but to be experienced directly by literally internalizing it. Drinking is a totalizing mode of perception associated with mediation.

In *Night* Faust longs repeatedly for such totalizing perception in terms of drinking and bathing. He wants to bathe himself whole in the dew of nature (397; the image recurs in lines 445–46). When the macrocosm seems to fail him he wants to drink directly from the breasts of nature (456). In the same scene he actually lifts the vial of poison to his lips, expecting to receive from it entry into a new life, and at the end of *Before the City Gate* he wants to drink the eternal light of the sun (1086). When Mephistopheles promises to satisfy his thirst for experience, it must be understood against this background. All drinking will be significant.

The spirits who sing Faust to sleep in the first *Study* scene devote the last section of their song to wine, and Mephistopheles takes Faust first of all to a tavern. Faust does not drink there, but we can see how Mephistopheles' wine—"spirits"—intensifies the experience of the drinkers, making them first "cannibalistic" (2293), then dreamers of beautiful vineyards (2316–19). In *Witch's Kitchen* Faust himself drinks for the first time in the play. The witch's potion, to be sure, seems a lot of hocus pocus, but Faust has first drunk in the image of the beautiful woman in the magic mirror. Drinking the potion repeats at the literal level what he has already done figuratively—internalized a powerful force. As in *Auerbach's Cellar*, the image has bifurcated, now into its figurative and literal versions. As a result it seems to parody itself: literal drinking is comic, but its significance is not.

The play has slipped into the Mephistophelean perspective on drinking, but soon enough it seems serious again. In Margarete's song about the King of Thule the king drinks at every feast from the "holy" (2777) goblet his dead mistress left him; his drinking thus takes on a quasireligious stature, for it signifies communion with the departed beloved. Act 1 of Part II continues in this vein, for wine is identified with gold when both are lacking in the emperor's household, and gold becomes a fluid. What is drunk is creative power, higher truth—but was this not already the significance of drinking in *Night*? Here the drinking imagery connects to the network of images clustered around gold and light.

THE FOUR ELEMENTS

The importance of the four elements in *Faust* derives from the ambience of Renaissance alchemy, in which the Faust legend is grounded. The line between magic and natural science was vaguer in the Renaissance than it is today, and magicians sought to control nature, embodied in the four elements earth, air, fire, and water. It is in terms of the four elements that Faust attempts to exorcise Mephistopheles (1271–91), and that the chorus of Helena's attendants dissolves back into nature at the end of act 3.

In Part I fire dominates; Mephistopheles has reserved it for himself (1377–78). At first it is unexceptionably conventional. He uses fire for all his little tricks, and from Auerbach's Cellar to the emperor's court, fire warns off those who fail to treat the devil's gifts with proper care. Nevertheless, as an element of nature, which is morally neutral, and as a form of light, fire is never exclusively devilish. The will-o'-the-wisp, for example, who leads Faust and Mephistopheles to the Walpurgis Night festival, may by tradition lead people astray, but he does lead Faust in the direction he wants to go and into a nature whose beauty Faust appreciates in normal romantic language. The wisp is a natural light and therefore participates in the quality of all other light in the play.

Water becomes as important as fire in Part II, especially in act 2, in which it becomes the home of incarnation—the element in which Zeus finds Leda and in which Homunculus finds Galatea. Water is the principle of life, Thales tells Homunculus, not fire; in act 1 Faust summoned mists to extinguish the fire that engulfed the court at the end of the masque. In some sense all of the water in act 2 is there to extinguish the fire in Faust, begun by the explosion set off by the shade of Helena at the end of act 1. Water functions as the equal and opposite reaction to fire.

Furthermore, the two elements frequently join. The most striking image of their synthesis is the rainbow in *Pleasant Landscape* at the beginning of Part II. There the light of the sun, "a sea of fire" (4710), illuminates the droplets of water thrown up by nature to create an inspiring reflection of human striving. The synthesis unravels into the emphasis on fire in act 1 and on water in act 2, but the two come together again in the epiphany of Galatea as Homunculus pours his flame into the water at her feet. The sirens hail water and fire, and everyone on stage joins in a salute to all four elements (8480–87). Helena, too, embodies the synthesis of fire and water, for she is the sun who rises to Faust out of the river Eurotas. This explicit emphasis on the union of fire and water in Part II also suggests in retrospect that all the wine in Part I, so consistently bursting into flame or otherwise associated with fire, is actually "fire-water." The interaction among these images constitutes another version of the play's dialectic.

Once an image becomes a virtual protagonist in the play, as fire and water seem to do, it alters its value in accordance with shifts in perspective, just as the characters do. As we have already seen, when Faust returns to a more Mephisthophelean mode in act 4 he decides that water is sterile and wants to keep it away. Even more surprising, Mephistopheles loses his final bid for Faust's soul when angels pelt him with burning roses, so that he is finally defeated by his own element. A similar, though not identical, instability emerges at the very end, when air suddenly becomes the element of divinity as the angels and Virgin float upward. The four elements remain always the expression of nature, but whose service they are in or what they represent specifically remains unfixed.

Almost any image in the play can be analyzed this way, and it will turn out to be tied to many others, yet also to pursue its own course. Directionality is an obvious example. The prologues talk repeatedly about erring and the erring path; at the same time the play zigzags between different perspectives and moods. Faust follows a zigzagging will-o'-the-wisp on Walpurgis Night, and his own path through the play zigzags from joy to despair, from nobility to deepest guilt, from mountain tops to deepest depths. At first movement upward seems to be good, to be toward truth, but Part I teaches Faust that he must move out into the world, not directly upward. Indeed, even in the *Prologue in Heaven* the natural motion of nature is circular. By the time Faust goes to the Mothers up or down makes no difference at all. At the end of the play he moves straight up again, but now surrounded by the circling boys, so that the sum of the motions is a spiral. As with the other images, there is a connection to a larger thematic network (here, erring), a joyous confusion of literal and figurative levels of signification, and a joyous confusion of perspectives. Like nature, Goethe's imagery is in constant motion, yet somehow orderly.

ALLUSION

Goethe often structures a single work as an extended allusion to another text, but in *Faust* the process seems to have run wild.

Through allusion, imitation, and parody *Faust* appropriates and reflects on an immense number of works and writers, including the Bible, Aeschylus, Sophocles, Euripides, Aristophanes, medieval poetry and morality drama, Dante, Shakespeare, Milton, the great Spanish dramatist Calderón de la Barca, the eighteenth-century English playwright Nicholas Rowe, paintings by Rembrandt, Raphael, Titian, and Carracci, and Roman and Renaissance statues. (This list is not exhaustive). Goethe also exploits a great variety of verse forms in *Faust*, each of which evokes its own historical period and literary genre.[12]

The range and density of allusions to other works, especially in Part II, astonishes and sometimes distresses readers today. Most of these allusions, however, were common knowledge to well-educated readers or spectators of the time. It is possible to follow Goethe, even through Part II, with little more than the standard classical texts read by schoolboys and the most commonly used German mythological dictionary of his day. The extensive commentary provided by editors from the late nineteenth century on documents the gap between the modern world and its own cultural tradition.

Like the images, Goethe's allusions are carefully patterned. Consider, for example, the classical allusions embedded in Part II. As the play moves from sixteenth-century Germany to Italian court masque to shades of Greek figures to Greece itself, the verse form adjusts, as does the way in which classical figures appear. During the court masque, for example, classical figures appear in unexpected shape (the Furies) or with their names and roles mixed up (the Fates), in garbled modern form, but by act 3 they appear concretely in their own historical forms. Goethe can achieve this because consistently in act 2, as the play moves further and further back into antiquity, a pattern of allusions to Renaissance and neoclassical texts and objects maintains our sense of historical distance from the aesthetic recreation of the past. The Mothers come from an essay by Plutarch, a very late classical writer. Erichtho, who speaks the prologue to the *Classical Walpurgis Night*, herself a figure from the late Latin writer Lucan, sounds remarkably like Shakespeare's Henry V on the night before the battle of Agincourt. Similarly, this pastiche of classical mythology ends with the triumph of Galatea, the subject of a painting by Raphael and also of the closing tableau of Calderón's 1635 play

Love the Greatest Enchantment. The framing of classical allusions by allusions from the period that rediscovered the classics maintains our historical distance, charts at every point our path back to the past, and prepares at the level of form the dialectic of past and present that is temporarily resolved in act 3. Not until James Joyce does another European writer exploit the classical tradition in such complex fashion.

We think of Goethe as a classicist, but Shakespeare is even more present in *Faust* than is the classical tradition. The consistent Shakespeareanizing in Part I reflects a programmatic effort to sub-stitute English models for French models of tragedy. More impor-tant, it offers models for what to do with Shakespeare, for there had been some disastrous experiments in Germany in the 1770s. Shakespearean drama had its own function at the end of the six-teenth century; to transplant it whole to the end of the eighteenth century was clearly inappropriate. By contextualizing Shakespeare with so many other dramatic forms, especially with so much oper-atic material, Goethe offers a different view from the formless wild genius his eighteenth-century contemporaries wanted to see, or from the psychologist par excellence that the nineteenth century made of him. The allusions to Puck and Ariel at the end of the *Walpurgis Night* and in act 1 imply a Shakespeare who embodies pure poetry, beyond any question of the stage at all. Goethe in fact came in his later years to see Shakespeare as too big for the stage—as a poet who wrote for the stage of the mind.

It is striking what a large proportion of the allusions, especially in Part I, are to other dramas. The nature of drama itself is called into question as the play evolves through such a variety of forms. Although Goethe subtitled *Faust* "A Tragedy," it conspicuously avoids the unified, psychologizing focus on an individual hero typical of eighteenth-century tragedy and of nineteenth-century realism. Goethe is evidently attempting in *Faust* to redefine tragedy from the pattern prevalent in his time by opening it up to alternative models embodied in Shakespeare, Renaissance masque, morality play, passion play, and opera. The allusions to painting and sculpture in Part II enhance this effect, for all the modes of drama that Goethe makes place for are allegorical and therefore more pictorial than conventional tragedy. Goethe's drama has less to do with creating an illusion of reality on the stage—the primary goal of drama as it developed in Europe in the eighteenth and nineteenth centuries—than with enabling drama to represent the relation of the human mind to what is not physically real. *Faust* transforms the theater of the world into the stage of the mind.

As Goethe's allusions accumulate, they imply, above and beyond the stories told by individual ones—such as the interaction with the origins of romantic thought implied by the repeated use of Rousseau, or the appropriate role of Shakespeare in German drama—that the tradition is present and important for its own sake. Goethe establishes his seriousness by tying his play to the history of European literature. He also establishes the only thing that can pass for objectivity in a post-Kantian world, for if the elements of his play echo what has come before, they cannot be only the solipsistic projection of an individual imagination. Finally, he uses allusions to historicize his own context and thus to remain conscious at all times of his own place in history and as history. Goethe's allusions underpin in the most essential way the different dialectics that constitute *Faust*, and at the same time explicitly draw attention to the ways in which *Faust* is shaped by, and itself shapes, the theater of the world.

appendix: plot summary

PART I

Dedication (1–32): A poet, presumably Goethe, addresses the wavering figures of his own text, who have approached him after a very long pause in the work. Memories of earlier years take possession of him, and he is inspired to write once more.

Prelude in the Theater (33–242): A director, a poet, and a harlequin argue about the play they are about to stage. The director wants action; the poet wants coherence and ideas; the player suggests combining both by drawing on real life, with its mixture of error and truth.

Prologue in Heaven (243–353): Three archangels celebrate the creation. Mephistopheles finds fault with it all, especially with mankind. He bets God that he can lead even His model servant Faust astray. God allows him to try.

Night (354–807): Faust, alone in his study, rejects all human knowledge and turns to magic. He longs to be outside with spirits in the moonlight, looks at and rejects the sign of the macrocosm, then invokes the earth spirit, who rejects him. After an interruption by his assistant Wagner, Faust becomes so depressed that he decides to take poison. His suicide is prevented by the Easter morning hymn from the neighboring church.

Before the City Gate (808–1177): On their Easter morning walk Faust and Wagner enjoy the spring and the festive citizens. A toast commemorating his unsuccessful efforts to avert the plague reminds Faust of his depression. He wishes he could follow the setting sun, then takes home with him a black poodle who has turned up.

Study (1178–1529): In calmer mood, Faust begins to translate the Gospel of St. John. The poodle swells in anger and finally turns out to be Mephistopheles, who introduces himself. Denied Faust's permission to leave, he has his spirits lull Faust to sleep and his rats help him escape.

Study II (1530–2072): Mephistopheles returns to find Faust again depressed. After cursing all of human life, Faust rejects a proffered pact on the grounds that the devil can offer nothing of lasting worth. Instead they make a wager: if Mephistopheles can ever make Faust wish for time to pause, then the devil can carry Faust off, body and soul. While Faust prepares to set off into the world, Mephistopheles offers a beginning student some misleading advice.

Auerbach's Cellar (2073–2336): Mephistopheles brings Faust to a famous tavern to observe the bestiality of the drinkers. After a few songs the devil makes the chosen wine of each flow from the table top. The drinkers become angry when some spilled wine turns to flame, but Mephistopheles covers Faust's escape by making them see visions.

Witch's Kitchen (2337–2604): Mephistopheles brings Faust to a witch's house to drink an elixir of youth. The witch is not at home, but her apes pretend to crown Mephistopheles king of the world while they wait. Faust meanwhile falls in love with the image of a beautiful woman in a magic mirror. The witch arrives, gives Faust his elixir with suitable incantations, and the two set off.

Street (2605–77): Faust exchanges one sentence with Margarete on the street and falls madly in love. He insists that Mephistopheles get her for him. The devil hesitates, but finally agrees to take Faust to her room while she is out and to fetch a gift for her.

Evening (2678–2804): As Margarete leaves her room, she wonders who Faust was. Faust and Mephistopheles enter, and Faust dreams ecstatically of his beloved. So moved is he by the purity and simplicity of her chamber that he hesitates to leave the casket of jewels

Mephistopheles has brought. Mephistopheles leaves it, and they escape as Margarete returns. She undresses, singing to herself, then finds the jewels.

Promenade (2805–64): Mephistopheles is angry because Margarete has shown the casket to her mother, who took it immediately to the priest. Faust sends Mephistopheles to get a better one.

The Neighbor's House (2865–3024): Margarete shows neighbor Martha the new casket and tries on some of the jewelry. Mephistopheles arrives and informs Martha that her husband has died. He asks permission to return in the evening with his friend to give more information to her and the young lady.

Street (3025–72): Faust is furious with Mephistopheles because he will have to lie about the death of Martha's husband in order to meet Margarete. Mephistopheles points out the inconsistency in Faust's position.

Garden (3073–3204): The two couples promenade in Martha's garden. Margarete and Faust charm one another; Mephistopheles narrowly avoids being caught by Martha.

A Garden House (3205–16): Faust and Margarete embrace but are immediately interrupted by Mephistopheles.

Forest and Cavern (3217–3373): Alone in the forest, Faust thanks the sublime spirit for fulfilling his desire for harmony with nature. As his mood shifts Mephistopheles arrives and berates him for not consummating his love for Margarete, who, he says, longs for Faust. Faust anticipates the tragic end of the affair.

Gretchen's Room (3374–3413): Margarete sits at her spinning wheel and longs for Faust.

Martha's Garden (3414–3543): Margarete catechizes Faust, who protests his sincere love for what she calls God. Margarete mistrusts Mephistopheles but admits her love for Faust. She agrees to drug her mother so that Faust can sleep with her.

At the Well (3544–86): Margarete listens to Lisa tell about an unmarried girl's pregnancy and how the others will punish her. Margarete wonders at her own changed situation.

Keep (3587–3619): Margarete prays to the Mater Dolorosa for help.

Night (3620–3775): Margarete's brother Valentine laments the shame that his sister has taken a lover. He attacks Mephistopheles after he sings a serenade beneath Margarete's window. Mephistopheles pushes Faust into the duel and assists him with magic. Faust wounds Valentine and flees. As he dies, Valentine tells his sister, before the assembled people, that she is a whore.

Cathedral (3776–3834): As Margarete listens to the Dies Irae in the cathedral, an evil spirit upbraids her for the death of her mother (from the sleeping potion) and her illegitimate pregnancy. She faints.

Walpurgis Night (3835–4222): Faust and Mephistopheles, led by a will-o'-the-wisp, enjoy the spring evening as they climb the Brocken (a mountain in the Harz) to celebrate the witches' sabbath. Groups of witches and warlocks pass them. Instead of going to see Satan at the summit, they stop at some campfires half-way up, where a sort of carnival is going on. Faust dances with a witch, but then is distracted by a vision of Margarete with a red line around her neck.

Walpurgis Night's Dream (4223–4398): Faust and Mephistopheles then watch a masque accompanied by an orchestra of insects in honor of the golden wedding anniversary of Oberon and Titania. At the end everything dissolves.

Gloomy Day: Field (prose): Faust is enraged that Margarete is about to be executed for killing their infant and insists that Mephistopheles save her. Mephistopheles agrees to carry her off if Faust can lead her from the prison.

Night: Open Field (4399–4404): As Faust and Mephistopheles gallop past, they see strange figures hovering around the gallows.

Dungeon (4405–4612): Faust finds Margarete insane in prison. When he calls her name she comes to her senses and wants to embrace him. He wants only to free her as quickly as possible. When he will not embrace her she renounces him, appeals to God, and refuses to leave. As Faust stands in desperation between her and Mephistopheles, the latter says she is condemned, and a voice from above says she is saved. Faust leaves with Mephistopheles as a voice from within calls after him.

PART II

Act I

Pleasant Landscape (4613–4727): Elves sing to the sleeping Faust to heal him from his bitter memories; the sun rises with great fanfare. Faust rejoices in the newly created world about him. As he turns from the blinding light of the rising sun he catches sight of a rainbow in the waterfall behind him and recognizes in it an image of human striving.

Imperial Palace: Throne Room (4728–5064): Mephistopheles is introduced as a new jester to replace the one who has just collapsed. The court complains to the emperor that money is lacking to maintain the luxury of the court and the order of the realm. Mephistopheles suggests there is plenty of buried treasure in the empire, if they will only seek it out. He prompts the court astrologer to second him. The emperor calls on all to celebrate Carnival while they wait for Mephistopheles' miracle to happen.

Spacious Hall (5065–5986): A herald introduces various figures in the processional masque with which the court celebrates Carnival. A strange group arrives which the herald does not recognize; they are Faust, disguised as Plutus, god of wealth, accompanied by Mephistopheles, disguised as Greed, and their own herald, Boy-Charioteer, who says he is Poetry. Boy-Charioteer flings jewels about, but they turn to insects as the greedy courtiers snatch at them. The emperor enters, disguised as Pan; he is so taken with the cauldron of gold offered by Plutus/Faust that he leans too far into it and his beard catches fire. Soon the entire hall is in flames, which Faust douses with a magical incantation.

Pleasure Garden (5987–6172): The emperor thanks Faust and Mephistopheles for their part in the entertainment. During the festival paper money, backed by the treasure beneath the earth, was printed, and it is now reviving the empire. Faust is named guardian of the new treasure.

Dark Gallery (6173–6306): The emperor has ordered Faust to show him Paris and Helen. Mephistopheles, who has no authority over classical ghosts, sends Faust to seek their shades from mysterious goddesses called the Mothers, who reside nowhere. Faust sets off.

Brightly Lit Halls (6307–76): While awaiting Faust's return, Mephistopheles offers court ladies cures for freckles and disappointed love.

Hall of Knights (6377–6565): Faust presents the shades of Paris and Helen on a specially prepared stage. The women admire Paris, the men Helen. Helen kisses Paris, who starts to carry her off. Faust, who has fallen in love with Helen, interferes, and the figures explode.

Act II

High-vaulted Narrow Gothic Room (6566–6818): Mephistopheles has brought Faust back to his old study, where nothing has changed since Part I. He reinterviews the student he advised in Part I, but the latter is now a know-all graduate and silences even the devil.

Laboratory (6819–7004): Wagner is busy making an artificial man. Mephistopheles arrives at the crucial moment, and the figure comes to life in its test tube. Mephistopheles asks for advice about Faust, who is lying senseless in the next room. Homunculus, as the figure is called, explains that Faust is dreaming of Leda and the swan and that he will only recover if he goes to Greece to attend the classical witches' sabbath.

CLASSICAL WALPURGIS NIGHT

Pharsalian Fields (7005–79): The classical witch Erichtho introduces the setting, then flees as Faust, Mephistopheles, and

Homunculus descend. Faust awakens as he touches Greek soil. The three agree to go their separate ways.

On the Upper Peneios (7080–7248): Mephistopheles encounters some sphinxes, who are too much for him. Faust arrives in search of Helen. The sphinxes send him to the centaur Chiron. Faust leaves, and the sphinxes send Mephistopheles on his way.

On the Lower Peneios (7249–7494): Faust comes upon the river god Peneios, surrounded by nymphs. He has a waking vision of Leda and the swan. Chiron comes and takes Faust on his back as they talk about Helen. Chiron brings him to the sibyl Manto, who will lead him into the Underworld as she did Orpheus.

On the Upper Peneios (7495–8033): An earthquake disturbs the sirens and sphinxes as a new mountain is raised by Seismos. Various creatures appear on the mountain and mine its gold. Soon they are all at war. Oblivious to this activity, Mephistopheles chases after classical witches, who upset him with their sudden transformations. He encounters Homunculus on the track of two Greek philosophers, who can, he hopes, tell him how to get a body. The first, Anaxagoras, tells him that all being originated in fire, and so he should become king of the little creatures on Seismos's mountain. The other, Thales, sees water as the principle of life and contradicts Anaxagoras' advice because of the war. The moon seems to fall down. In fact, the moon is still there, but the mountain is gone, creatures and all. Thales and Homunculus set off for the sea, while Mephistopheles finds his way to the cave of the Phorcyads, who delight him. These three hags, who share one eye and tooth among them, agree to lend Mephistopheles their form if he provides his own eye and tooth. Mephistopheles turns into Phorcyas.

Rocky Coves of the Aegean Sea (8034–8487): Thales brings Homunculus to the shore, where sirens, Nereids and other creatures have gathered with Nereus, the old man of the sea. Because he is waiting for the annual visit of his daughter Galatea, who has succeeded Venus as goddess of beauty, Nereus advises Homunculus to seek out Proteus. Homunculus and Thales find Proteus, who is fascinated with Homunculus in his test tube. Proteus advises him to enter the sea and evolve up the chain of being. A procession passes, followed by Galatea herself, who exchanges loving greetings with her father as she flashes by. Homunculus throws himself into the waves at her feet, his test tube breaks on her shell-chariot, and the water around her glows with the flames of love. All present join in an ecstatic celebration of the four elements.

Act III

Before the Palace of Menelaus at Sparta (8488–9126): Helena enters with her chorus of captured Trojan women. They have just arrived from Troy and been sent ahead to prepare a sacrifice. Phorcyas (Mephistopheles) comes out of the palace, convinces them that they themselves are the intended sacrifice, and offers them safety in the castle of a northern visitor who moved in while Menelaus was at Troy. They accept.

Inner Courtyard (9127–9573): Faust welcomes Helena to his castle in the guise of a medieval crusader. She joins him on his throne and, intrigued with his language, learns to speak in rhyme. The watchman Lynceus interrupts their love scene to warn that Menelaus and his men are coming. Faust describes an Arcadian place of safety, and the stage transforms itself.

Shady Grove (9574–10038): Phorcyas tells the chorus that Faust and Helena have a newborn son who is growing up from moment to moment. The chorus is reminded of the Greek god Hermes. Music starts to play, and Faust, Helena, and their son, Euphorion, appear. Euphorion's excessive liveliness worries his loving parents, but he cannot be restrained. He tries to embrace a maiden from the chorus, then climbs a rocky cliff. From the top he sees a war in the world outside and wants to join in. He tries to fly off and falls to earth. The music stops. Helena will follow Euphorion to the Under-world. As Faust embraces Helena she dissolves, and her clothing turns into a cloud that carries Faust off. The chorus returns to the four elements, and Phorcyas reveals herself to be Mephistopheles.

Act IV

High Mountains (10039–344): The cloud deposits Faust in Germany; Mephistopheles joins him and offers him whatever lands he pleases. Faust chooses the shore of the sea; he wants to wall out the water and open new land.

In the Foothills (10345–782): He and Mephistopheles go to the camp of the emperor, who is engaged in civil war. Mephistopheles wins the battle by using illusions.

The Counter-Emperor's Tent (10783–11042): Mephistopheles' supernatural helpers loot the enemy's tent. The court arrives. In reward for his services Faust is granted the seashore as his fief. The rest of the recovered empire is divided up, and the emperor is no better off than before.

Act V

Open Landscape (11043–142): A visitor hears from the old couple Baucis and Philemon how Faust's land-recovery projects have succeeded. Now they are frightened because Faust wants their small holdings to complete his empire.

Palace (11143–287): An aged, wealthy Faust is frustrated because the highest point in his domains still belongs to the old couple. Mephistopheles and his assistants bring treasure back from their latest trading excursion, which is indistinguishable from piracy, but Faust can think only about the land of the old people. He orders Mephistopheles to move them to a new house.

Deep Night (11288–383): Lynceus, Faust's watchman, celebrates the beauty of the world, then describes with horror how the house of Baucis and Philemon burns to the ground. Mephistopheles comes and reports that unfortunately, the couple resisted and could not be saved. Faust is appalled.

Midnight (11384–510): Four grey women approach to haunt Faust. Want, Debt, and Misery are unable to penetrate his wealth, but Care slips in through the keyhole. Faust resists her and in the process renounces magic. She blinds him, and Faust reacts by summoning forth his men to work.

Great Courtyard of the Palace (11511–603): Mephistopheles and his ghosts come out and dig Faust's grave. Believing that they are digging a drainage ditch, Faust celebrates his great achievement. In anticipation of the eternal struggles of the community that will live on his reclaimed land, Faust claims to enjoy the highest moment and pronounces the words that he bet Mephistopheles he would never say. He falls to the ground.

Entombment (11604–843): Mephistopheles and his henchmen surround Faust's corpse so that they can snatch the soul the moment it ventures out. Angels fly in, strewing roses, which the devils' hot breath ignites. Touched by the burning roses, Mephistopheles falls in love with the handsome angels who carry Faust's soul away.

Mountain Gorges (11844–12111): Hermits celebrate divine love and nature in a mountainous landscape. The angels fly in with Faust's soul and join the celebration. The Mater Gloriosa (Holy Virgin) floats up through the landscape, surrounded by various penitent women from the New Testament and the soul of Margarete. The latter wants to instruct the soul of Faust; the Mater Gloriosa tells her she should rise, and the soul of Faust will doubtless follow. A mystical chorus celebrates what has just been enacted.

notes and references

1. *Campaign in France, Gesamtausgabe der Werke und Schriften in zweiundzwanzig Bänden*, vol. 10 (Stuttgart, Germany: Cotta, 1960), 321.

2. *Goethes Faust*, commentary by Erich Trunz (Hamburg, Germany: Wegner, 1963), 421.

3. *De l'Allemagne*, vol. 1 (Paris: Garnier-Flammarion, 1968), 343.

4. Explicated by Jeffrey Russell in *Mephistopheles: The Devil in the Modern World* (Ithaca, N.Y.: Cornell University Press, 1986), 128–67.

5. *Oeuvres Complètes*, vol. 1 (Paris: Gallimard, 1959), 1046.

6. *Gesamtausgabe der Werke und Schriften in zweiundzwanzig Bänden*, vol. 8 (1952), 414–16.

7. Frances A. Yates documents this situation in *Theatre of the World* (Chicago: University of Chicago Press, 1969), 30–32 and 51–52.

8. *Gesamtausgabe der Werke und Schriften in zweiundzwanzig Bänden*, vol. 15 (n.d.), 755.

9. See Colleen McDannell and Bernhard Lang, *Heaven: A History* (New Haven, Conn.: Yale University Press, 1988), 183.

10. *Maxims and Reflections*, no. 241: "Der Handelnde ist immer gewissenlos; es hat niemand Gewissen als der Betrachtende." Aphorisms were an important mode of expression for Goethe. Unfortunately, no translations of his collection are currently available.

11. *Maxims and Reflections*, no. 915:

> Das ganze Leben besteht aus
> Wollen und Nicht-Vollbringen,
> Vollbringen und Nicht-Wollen.

12. The allusions are discussed in some detail scene-by-scene in Jane K. Brown, *Goethe's Faust: The German Tragedy* (Ithaca, N.Y.: Cornell University Press, 1986).

selected bibliography

PRIMARY WORKS

Faust. Edited by Cyrus Hamlin, translated by Walter Arndt. New York: Norton, 1976. Accurate translation of both parts; preserves meter and rhyme; excellent commentary and apparatus.

_____. Translated by Walter Kaufman. New York: Doubleday, 1961. Part I and selections from Part II (*Pleasant Landscape* and act 5); German on facing pages.

_____. Translated by David Luke. New York: Oxford University Press, 1987. Part I only.

_____. Translated by Philip Wayne. Harmondsworth, England: Penguin, Part I 1949, Part II 1959. Both parts in two volumes; preserves meter; accurate and readable.

Goethe's Collected Works. Edited by Victor Lange, Eric Blackall, and Cyrus Hamlin. New York: Suhrkamp, 1983–89. 12 vols., as follows:

Vol. 1, *Selected Poems.* Edited by Christopher Middleton; translated by Michael Hamburger, David Luke, Christopher Middleton, John Frederick Nims, and Vernon Watkins.

Vol. 2, *Faust I & II.* Edited and translated by Stuart Atkins. Preserves meter, exceptionally readable.

Vol. 3, *Essays on Art and Literature.* Edited by John Gearey; translated by Ellen and Ernest H. von Nardroff.

Vols. 4 and 5, *From My Life: Poetry and Truth, Campaign in France 1792, and Siege of Mainz.* Edited by Thomas P. Saine and Jeffrey L. Sammons; translated by Robert R. Heitner and Thomas P. Saine.

Vol. 6, *Italian Journey.* Edited by Thomas P. Saine and Jeffrey L. Sammons; translated by Robert R. Heitner.

Vol. 7, *Early Verse Drama and Prose Plays.* Edited by Cyrus Hamlin and Frank Ryder; translated by Robert M. Browning, Michael Hamburger, Cyrus Hamlin, and Frank Ryder.

Vol. 8, *Verse Plays and Epic.* Edited by Cyrus Hamlin and Frank Ryder; translated by Michael Hamburger, Hunter Hannum, and David Luke.

Vol. 9: *Wilhelm Meister's Apprenticeship.* Edited by Eric A. Blackall; translated by Eric A. Blackall in cooperation with Victor Lange.

Vol. 10, *Conversations of German Refugees* and *Wilhelm Meister's Journey-man Years*. Edited by Jane K. Brown; *Conversations* translated by Jan van Heurck in cooperation with Jane K. Brown; *Wilhelm Meister* by Krishna Winston.
Vol. 11, *The Sorrows of Young Werther, Elective Affinities,* and *Novella*. Edited by David E. Wellbery; translated by Victor Lange and Judith Ryan.
Vol. 12, *Scientific Studies*. Edited and translated by Douglas Miller.

SECONDARY WORKS

Books and Parts of Books

Atkins, Stuart P. *Goethe's Faust: A Literary Analysis*. Cambridge: Harvard University Press, 1958. The most influential close reading of *Faust* as a tragedy of character; covers both parts.
_____. "Motif in Literature: The Faust Theme." In *Dictionary of the History of Ideas*. Vol. 3, 244–53. New York: Scribners, 1973.
Berman, Marshall. *All That Is Solid Melts into Air: The Experience of Modernity*. New York: Simon & Schuster, 1982. Substantial portion of book deals with *Faust*.
Brown, Jane K. *Goethe's Faust: The German Tragedy*. Ithaca, N.Y.: Cornell University Press, 1986. Close reading of both parts, focusing on imagery, allusions, and questions of genre.
Burke, Kenneth. "Goethe's *Faust*, Part I" and "*Faust II*—The Ideas behind the Imagery." In *Language as Symbolic Action: Essays on Life, Literature, and Method*, 139–62 and 163–85. Berkeley: University of California Press, 1966.
Cassirer, Ernst. *Rousseau, Kant and Goethe*. Translated by James Gutmann, Paul Oskar Kristeller, and John Hermann Randall, Jr. New York: Harper & Row, 1963.
Citati, Pietro. *Goethe*. Translated by Raymond Rosenthal. New York: Dial, 1974. Almost half of book is on *Faust*.
Cottrell, Alan P. *Goethe's Faust: Seven Essays*. University of North Carolina Studies in the Germanic Languages and Literatures, no. 86. Chapel Hill: University of North Carolina Press, 1976. Separate essays on particular topics in Parts I and II.
Cottrell, Alan P. *Goethe's View of Evil and the Search for a New Image of Man in Our Time*. Edinburgh, Scotland: Floris, 1982.
Fairley, Barker. *Goethe's Faust: Six Essays*. Oxford, England: Clarendon Press, 1953.
Friedenthal, Richard. *Goethe: His Life and Times*. 3 vols. Cleveland: World, 1963. Readable debunking of older Goethe-worship.

Gearey, John. *Goethe's Faust: The Making of Part I*. New Haven, Conn.: Yale University Press, 1981. Thorough description of the complex genesis of Part I.

Gillies, Alexander. *Goethe's Faust: An Interpretation*. Oxford, England: Blackwell, 1957.

Graham, Ilse. *Goethe: A Portrait of the Artist*. Berlin: de Gruyter, 1977.

Haile, Harry G. *Invitation to Goethe's Faust*. University: Alabama University Press, 1978. Clear introduction to basic themes of both parts.

Hamlin, Cyrus, ed. *Faust*. Norton Critical Edition. New York: Norton, 1976. Includes translations of some of Goethe's most important statements about *Faust*, contemporary reactions to *Faust*, and useful critical essays about the play.

Jantz, Harold. *The Form of Faust: The Work of Art and Its Intrinsic Structures*. Baltimore: Johns Hopkins University Press, 1978. Good presentation of main themes.

Lange, Victor, ed. *Goethe: A Collection of Critical Essays*. Englewood Cliffs, N.J.: Prentice-Hall, 1968. Introductory essays.

Leppmann, Wolfgang. *The German Image of Goethe*. Oxford, England: Clarendon Press, 1961.

Lewes, George Henry. *The Life and Works of Goethe*. 3d ed. 2 vols. London: Smith & Elder, 1875 (1st ed. 1855, 2d ed. 1864). First full biography; still useful and readable.

McMillan, Douglas J. *Approaches to Teaching Goethe's Faust*. New York: Modern Language Association of America, 1987.

Mason, Eudo C. *Goethe's Faust: Its Genesis and Purport*. Berkeley: University of California Press, 1967. Cogent analysis of Part I, focused on Mephistopheles.

Vickery, John B., and J'nan Sellery, eds. *Goethe's Faust, Part One: Essays in Criticism*. Belmont, Calif.: Wadsworth, 1969. Significant essays on aspects of Part I; little overlap with essays in Hamlin edition.

Wilkinson, Elizabeth M., and Leonard A. Willoughby. *Goethe: Poet and Thinker*. New York: Barnes & Noble, 1962.

Williams, John R. *Goethe's Faust*. London: Allen & Unwin, 1987. Commentary on both parts.

Articles

Bennett, Benjamin. "'Vorspiel auf dem Theater': the Ironic Basis of Goethe's *Faust*." *German Quarterly* 49 (1976): 438–55.

Brown, Jane K. "Mephistopheles the Nature Spirit." *Studies in Romanticism* 24 (1985), 475–90.

Flax, Neil M. "The Presence of the Sign in Goethe's *Faust*." *PMLA* 98 (1983): 183–203.

index

Index

the author

Jane K. Brown has published extensively on Goethe and on problems of genre in drama. Her books include *Goethe's Faust: The German Tragedy* (1986) and *Goethe's Cyclical Narratives* (1975). She has edited *Wilhelm Meisters Wanderjahre* in English and published essays on Goethe, Droste-Hülshoff, and Shakespeare. She is president of the Goethe Society of North America and has served as book review editor of the society's *Yearbook*. Currently chair of the Department of Germanics and professor of Germanics and comparative literature at the University of Washington, she has also taught English at the University of Colorado and German at the University of Virginia, Mount Holyoke College, and the University of New Hampshire. She earned her B.A. from Harvard University and her Ph.D. from Yale.